On this day . . . let thy food
be prepared with singleness of heart
that thy fasting may be perfect,
or, in other words,
that thy joy may be full.

Doctrine and Covenants 59:13

WITH
SINGLENESS OF HEART
Recipes for Sunday Meals

Helen R. Bateman
JoAnn E. Hickman
Jane S. Eddington

Illustrations by Kathy Bateman Peterson
Cover photography by Ramon Winegar

Deseret Book Company
Salt Lake City, Utah
1984

ISBN 0-87747-731-0
Library of Congress Catalog Card Number 84-71871

First printing September 1984

CONTENTS

PREFACE

In the Mary and Martha story in Luke 10:38-42, the Lord shows us something vital. Martha, bustling about with the kitchen duties, was feeling a bit resentful as Mary, adoring and learning from the Savior's wisdom, seemed to shirk her tasks. Martha complained, and Jesus answered with mild chastisement: "Martha, Martha, thou art careful and troubled about many things: But one thing is needful: and Mary hath chosen that good part, which shall not be taken away from her."

How can we hold to the spiritual, like Mary, and yet do Martha's essential tasks too? We humans are a mixture, with both physical and spiritual needs to feed. How do we learn the proper balance? Our Father knew that mortals would have strong physical pressures, and so He gave us a gift of time, a day set aside for spiritual regeneration: the Sabbath.

Moses and the children of Israel were commanded to labor six days in order to survive physically in the world, and then to rest on the seventh day in order to survive spiritually. To young homemakers with the constant demands of little children, to church workers with many responsibilities who find Sunday their busiest day, and to all others in demanding circumstances, the commandment to rest seems impossible. Yet this is rest in its narrow definition. If we view it as an opportunity to create in our lives a spiritual renewal in the "rest of the Lord," a time to fortify our souls for the return on Monday to the everyday working world, then we can foster an attitude that will make it possible and still accomplish our necessary physical chores. To experience the "rest of the Lord" is to feel the presence of the Lord.

What a wellspring of strength and celebration Sunday could be if we truly used that holy day to feast on the spiritual food as the Lord has commanded! Brigham Young reminds us: "The Lord has planted within us a divinity; and that divine immortal spirit requires to be fed. Will earthly food answer for that purpose? No; it will only keep this body alive as long as the spirit stays with it, which gives us an opportunity of doing good." (*Journal of Discourses* 7:138.)

And yet we cannot totally set aside our physical needs. Part of honoring the Sabbath demands that our homes be at their best, our clothes be at their best, our thoughts and ideas and food be at their very best. The key for this is preparation ahead, like the children of Israel who collected manna for the coming Sabbath and found it sweet to the taste. Then, if we truly want to come into His rest, our Mary's hearts can partake of the spiritual Sabbath feast even as we taste of the physical feast our Martha's hands have prepared.

This cookbook had its birth as we three good friends reminisced about the Sunday dinners of our childhood, not only the good food but also the family togetherness and love, free from weekday routine and pressures. The wonderful sharing of hopes and dreams as we lingered for long conversations around the table melded our families into closeness. How empty that table seemed when even one person was missing, and how thrilling it was when those who were married or away from home rejoined our table!

We truly believe that Sunday dinner should be a spiritual high point of the week. No event could be more symbolic of family unity than breaking bread together after church. Family prayer at the dinner table seems to have a special poignancy on the Sabbath day, as we thank the Lord for blessings and seek His guidance for the week ahead.

Our concern that these lofty goals are often lost in drudgery prompted us to write this book. Included are many of our favorite recipes, good dishes that we have prepared for our own families and have enjoyed sharing with others. In keeping with our Sabbath goals, most of the dishes can be prepared in advance, and in many of the recipes we have noted the point at which the dishes can be refrigerated or frozen. If the dish is placed in the oven directly from the refrigerator or freezer, you should add a few minutes to the baking time. Dishes that must be prepared on Sunday are planned to involve very simple preparation and little time.

That your mind might be lifted as your hands serve, we have also included a collection of our favorite sayings, to serve as food for your thought while you cook. May you be able to unite the best of both Mary and Martha as you strive to serve "with singleness of heart"!

Helen R. Bateman   *JoAnn E. Hickman*   *Jane S. Eddington*

About the Authors

The authors of *With Singleness of Heart* all live in the same neighborhood in Provo, Utah, and are all active in Relief Society and other auxiliary organizations of The Church of Jesus Christ of Latter-day Saints.

Helen Ream Bateman has a bachelor's degree in home economics and a master's degree in education, both from Brigham Young University. For many years she taught family life education at Provo High School. The author of *Roots and Wings: A Book of Family Traditions*, also published by Deseret Book, she is married to Dr. LaVar Bateman, professor of speech at BYU. They have five children.

JoAnn Emmett Hickman, a native of Logan, Utah, received a bachelor's degree in elementary education from Utah State University. She has lived in many parts of the world, as her husband, Dr. Martin Hickman, was in foreign service for several years. He is now dean of the College of Family, Home, and Social Services at BYU. The Hickmans have six daughters.

Jane S. Eddington has traveled extensively all her married life and is noted as an excellent hostess and cook. Her husband, Robert, is a retired pilot with the U.S. Air Force and has directed Red Cross activities in Provo. Most recently they have been serving as missionaries in Samoa. They have two sons and two daughters.

Kathy Bateman Peterson, a daughter of Helen Bateman, illustrated the book. She resides in Ephraim, Utah, and has four children.

A merry heart hath a continual feast

Beef, Lamb, Pork, Poultry, and Seafood

Beef

The Sunday Roast	3
Gingered Short Ribs or Pot Roast	3
Beef Rouladen	3
Swiss Steak	4
Beef Stroganoff	4
Sukiyaki	4
Polynesian Beef	5
Green Pepper Steak	5
Sweet and Sour Sunday Stew	5
Beef-Broccoli Stir Fry	6
Eight-hour Stew	6
Curried Beef	6
Indian Meat Loaf	6
Polynesian Meatballs	7
Meatballs and Rice	7
Swedish Sour Cream Meatballs	7
Tiny Meatballs	8
Bitochki	8
Beef Noodles Supreme	8
Five-Spice Casserole	9
Enchilada Casserole	9
Tamale Pie	9
Sunday Delight	9
Lasagne	10
Florentine Lasagne	10
Beef, Noodles, and Beans Italiano	10
Stuffed Cabbage Rolls	11
Stuffed Zucchini	11
Paul Bunyans	11
Mexican Pile-up	12

Lamb

Alsatian Lamb and Pork Bake	12
Sunday Lamb Stew	13
Barbecued Leg of Lamb	13

Pork

All-night Pork Bake	13
Pork Roast with Sauerkraut	13
Pork Shoulder Pot Roast	14
Stuffed Pork Chops Supreme	14
Pork Piquant	14
Ham Skillet Dinner	15
Ham or Chicken Amandine	15
Torta Prima Vera	15
Tonnarelli	16
Pan Quiche	16
Sausage and Eggs Continental	16

Poultry

Chicken Adobo	17
Garlic Fried Chicken	17
Quick Yummy Chicken	17
Barbecued Chicken	17
Portuguese Chicken	18
Orange-glazed Chicken	18
Elegant Stuffed Chicken	18
Chicken Macadamia	18
Chicken and Dried Beef Casserole	19
Chicken Mincemeat	19
Lemon Chicken	19
Florentine Chicken	19
Chicken Chow Mein	20
Chicken Olé	20
Almond Chicken Rice Bake	20
Dinner's in the Oven	21
Sausage-stuffed Chicken Roll	21
Hot Chicken Salad	22
Chicken Logs	22
Jalapeño Chicken Enchiladas	22
Chicken Tamale Pie	23
Turkey Barbecue	23
Turkey Tetrazzini	23

Seafood

Crab and Shrimp Casserole	24
Crab Diablo	24
Seafood Casserole	24
Seafood Lasagne	25
Crab Casserole	25

BEEF

The Sunday Roast

Probably the easiest meat to prepare and the favorite of most families is the Sunday roast. Almost any cut of beef is tender and delicious if cooked long and slowly enough. If you want beef that can be served rare (such as prime rib or sirloin tip), you might want to save such a roast for holidays or days when you can be at home to time the meat precisely.

For cuts such as shoulder, heel, seven-bone, round, or rump, put the meat in a roaster or casserole and season with salt and pepper. Do not brown the meat and do not add any water. Cover and place in a slow oven (225 to 275° F., depending on size of the roast and when it is to be served). A 4- to 5-pound roast put into the oven at 8:00 A.M. should be ready between noon and 1:00 P.M. The roast will be brown, fork-tender, and there will be plenty of nice juice for gravy. If you wish a darker gravy, remove the roast to a platter and boil down the juice to a deep, brown color; add water and thicken.

To truly prepare your Sunday roast with "singleness of heart," on Saturday evening peel a small onion and a potato for each family member and cut 4 or 5 carrots into large pieces. Keep the vegetables in cold water overnight. Some nutrients are lost this way, but occasionally it is worth it. Drain the vegetables Sunday morning and put them in with the meat.

Variations

German style: Add 3 or 4 medium dill pickles and 1 teaspoon dill weed.

Italian style: Add 1 small can (8 ounces) tomato sauce, 1 teaspoon oregano, and 1 teaspoon basil.

French style: Add 1 cup fresh sliced mushrooms or 1 can (8 ounces) mushrooms, 1 pound peeled onions, and 1 cup grape juice.

Family favorite: Season with 1 package dry onion soup mix.

Gingered Short Ribs or Pot Roast

> 3 pounds beef short ribs or pot roast
> ¼ cup flour
> ½ teaspoon salt
> 1 teaspoon powdered ginger
> 1½ cups chopped onions
> 1½ cups chopped celery
> 1 clove garlic, minced
> ½ cup catsup
> 1 tablespoon soy sauce
> 1 can (12 ounces) ginger ale

Combine flour, salt, and ginger. Dredge meat in flour mixture and remove, saving remaining flour. Brown meat in a heavy skillet in a small amount of fat. Place meat in a large casserole dish or roasting pan. Sauté onions, celery, and garlic 2 to 3 minutes in remaining fat. Add reserved flour mixture and blend. Add catsup, soy sauce, and ginger ale. Pour over meat; cover. (Can be refrigerated at this point.) Bake until tender, about 3 hours at 250° F. or shorter time at higher temperature. Serves 6 to 8.

Beef Rouladen

> Boneless beef tip or round roast
> Prepared mustard
> Chopped onions
> Diced bacon
> Quartered dill pickle spears
> Chopped parsley
> Salt and pepper
> Shortening
> ⅓ cup cream or sour cream

Have butcher slice thinly the boneless beef tip or roast. Cut meat slices into pieces each about 4" x 6". Allow about 1½ pieces meat per serving.

Spread mustard on each piece of meat. Place 1 teaspoon each of onions and diced bacon across center of slice. Lay 1 pickle spear on top, and sprinkle with a little parsley and salt and pepper. Roll up and secure with toothpicks. Melt shortening in roasting pan, and brown meat rolls in shortening. (Can be refrigerated at this point.) Add 1 cup water to meat in roasting pan. Cover and bake in slow oven (about 250° F.) 2 to 3 hours. Remove meat to a warm platter and make gravy with drippings. Just before serving, stir cream or sour cream into gravy and heat; do not boil. Serve with mashed or boiled potatoes and German Red Cabbage (see index).

Swiss Steak

8 pieces round steak
4 tablespoons flour
½ teaspoon salt
4 tablespoons butter
2 large onions, sliced and separated into rings
1 cup sliced fresh mushrooms or 1 can (4 ounces) mushrooms
1 cup beef bouillon or the liquid from canned mushrooms plus 1 bouillon cube and enough water to make 1 cup
Garlic salt to taste
½ cup evaporated milk or half-and-half

Combine flour and salt; reserve 1 tablespoon and rub the remaining 3 tablespoons into the meat. Melt butter in a skillet and brown the steak on both sides. Transfer meat to a baking dish. Lay onion rings on top of meat. Brown the mushrooms lightly in the meat juice in skillet; stir in reserved 1 tablespoon flour. Add bouillon, garlic salt, and evaporated milk or half-and-half. Cook over low heat, stirring constantly, until slightly thickened. Pour over meat and onion. Cover. (Can be refrigerated at this point.) Bake at 325° F. for 1½ hours or at 225° F. for 3 hours. Serves 8.

Beef Stroganoff

2 pounds lean boneless beef
2 tablespoons butter
1 tablespoon minced onion
½ teaspoon salt
¼ teaspoon nutmeg
½ pound fresh mushrooms, sliced
1 cup sour cream

Slice beef into thin strips across the grain. Melt butter in a heavy skillet; add onion and cook until transparent. Add beef strips; sprinkle with salt and nutmeg. Cook beef quickly, stirring, until brown on all sides. Add mushrooms and cook for 1 to 2 minutes. Add sour cream and stir until heated; don't boil. Serve over rice or noodles. Serves 6. *Note:* Because the beef cooks so quickly, this is a main dish you prepare at the last minute on Sunday.

Nothing is worth more than this day. (Goethe)

Sukiyaki

1½ pounds well-trimmed lean beef
1 pound fresh bean sprouts or 1 can (16 ounces) bean sprouts, drained and rinsed
1 cup French-cut frozen or fresh green beans
1 cup celery cut on diagonal in thin slices
1 cup fresh mushrooms
1 can (5 ounces) water chestnuts, sliced, or bamboo shoots
1 small crookneck yellow squash, cut in thin slices
6 green onions, cut in 1-inch pieces
1 carrot, cut in thin slices
Cooking oil
Sugar
Soy sauce

Cut the meat into paper-thin slices, each about 1" x 2". (If you partially freeze the meat, it will be easier to slice.) Put in a bowl, cover, and store in refrigerator. Prepare all the vegetables and store separately in plastic bags, tightly closed.

When ready to serve, arrange a large tray with meat in the center and vegetables arranged in individual piles around the outside. Put oil, soy sauce, and a small bowl of sugar on another small tray. When guests are seated, prepare the sukiyaki on the dinner table or a small table nearby. Heat an electric frying pan or wok on high, and pour in a little oil. Add about one-third of the meat and sprinkle with a little sugar and soy sauce, stirring meat with chopsticks. Add one-third of each of the vegetables and cook, stirring, until vegetables are tender-crisp.

Serve over steaming hot rice. Repeat process twice, cooking one-third at a time. Serves 8 to 10.

Note: Almost any vegetable can be used in sukiyaki—these are only a suggestion. Fry any combination of your favorites. Yams are delicious, but they should not be overcooked; cook only until crisp. If desired, break a small raw egg in each bowl and stir with chopsticks; then add hot rice (egg will cook when rice is stirred in).

Polynesian Beef

    2½ pounds sirloin tip, cut thin across grain
        into 2½" x 1" strips
    1½ teaspoons garlic salt
    1 teaspoon paprika
    1 teaspoon ginger
    2 tablespoons cooking oil
    ½ cup diced celery
    2 medium onions, diced
    ½ cup diced green pepper
    2 medium tomatoes, chopped
    1 can (20 ounces) pineapple chunks
    1 can (10 ounces) condensed beef broth
    3 tablespoons brown sugar
    ¼ cup wine vinegar
    2 tablespoons soy sauce
    ¼ cup water
    3 tablespoons cornstarch

Combine garlic salt, ginger, and paprika; coat meat with mixture. In a large skillet, brown a small amount of meat at a time in hot oil. Remove pieces as cooked and drain. Set meat aside. In oil remaining in skillet, cook celery, onions, and green pepper until tender-crisp. Add meat, tomatoes, pineapple (including juice), beef broth, brown sugar, and vinegar; heat. Combine soy sauce, water, and cornstarch; stir into meat and vegetable mixture, and boil 1 minute. Serve over hot cooked rice. Serves 8 to 10.

Green Pepper Steak

    1½ pounds round steak, cut in strips ½ inch
        thick
    ¼ cup flour
    ½ teaspoon salt
    ⅛ teaspoon pepper
    ¼ cup cooking oil
    1 can (8 ounces) or 1 cup tomatoes (reserve liquid)
    1¾ cups water
    ½ cup chopped onion
    1 small clove garlic, minced
    1 tablespoon dried beef gravy base (optional)
    1½ teaspoons Worcestershire sauce
    2 large green peppers, cut into strips

Combine flour, salt, and pepper in paper bag; add meat and shake until well coated. In a large skillet, cook meat in oil until browned on all sides. Drain tomatoes and set aside. Add liquid from tomatoes, water, onion, garlic, and gravy base to meat in skillet; cover and simmer about 1¼ hours, until meat is tender. (May be refrigerated at this point.) Reheat, covered. Stir in Worcestershire sauce and green peppers. Cover and simmer for about 5 minutes. If necessary, thicken gravy with a mixture of a little flour and cold water. Add drained tomatoes. Heat and serve over hot cooked rice. Serves 6 to 8.

Sweet and Sour Sunday Stew

    2 pounds boneless lean beef chuck,
        cut in 1-inch cubes
    2 tablespoons cooking oil
    1 cup catsup
    ½ cup brown sugar
    ½ cup wine vinegar
    1 tablespoon Worcestershire sauce
    2 cups water
    1 large onion, chopped
    4 large carrots, cut into ¾-inch chunks
    4 small onions, peeled
    4 large potatoes, cubed

In a large, heavy skillet or Dutch oven, brown beef cubes in oil. Combine catsup, brown sugar, vinegar, Worcestershire sauce, water, and chopped onion; pour over beef. Add carrots and small whole onions. Simmer until vegetables and meat are tender, about 2½ hours. Add potatoes and simmer until tender, about 30 minutes. Thicken gravy, if necessary, with a small amount of flour mixed with cold water. (May be refrigerated at this point, and reheated just before serving.) Serve with garlic bread. Makes 6 to 8 servings.

Beef-Broccoli Stir Fry

1½ pounds broccoli
½ teaspoon monosodium glutamate (optional)
1 pound boneless beef round steak or chuck,
    cut across grain in thin strips
2 tablespoons cooking oil
2 cups fresh bean sprouts
6 green onions, cut in ¼-inch pieces
1 clove of garlic, minced
1 teaspoon grated fresh ginger or
    ½ teaspoon ground ginger
½ cup water
¼ cup soy sauce or to taste
1 tablespoon cornstarch

Slice broccoli stems into rounds ¼-inch thick. Cut tops into flowerettes. Set aside. Sprinkle monosodium glutamate on meat. In a wok or large fry pan, quickly brown the meat, one-half at a time, in hot oil. Remove meat and set aside. Add broccoli and bean sprouts and cook until tender-crisp. Add onions, garlic, and ginger and stir fry 1 minute. Combine water, soy sauce, and cornstarch. Add to vegetables and cook until thickened. Stir in meat and heat. Serve with hot cooked rice. Serves 6 to 8. *Note:* This is also good made with ground beef.

Eight-hour Stew

2 pounds boneless beef, cut into 1½-inch cubes*
3 tablespoons instant tapioca
4 carrots, cut in chunks
3 or 4 ribs celery, cut in diagonal slices
1 large onion, cut in wedges
1 quart or 2 cans (16 ounces each) tomatoes
1 cup fresh bread crumbs
1 scant tablespoon salt
Pepper to taste
Pinch of basil or marjoram
5 potatoes, cut in quarters
1 package (10 ounces) frozen peas

Put meat in a buttered Dutch oven or heavy roasting pan. Add in layers the tapioca, carrots, celery, onion, tomatoes, bread crumbs, salt, pepper, and basil or marjoram. Cover and bake at 225° F. for 5 to 8 hours. Twenty minutes before serving, cook the potatoes in a small amount of water until tender. Drain, butter, and season; spread over the top of the stew. Cook peas for one minute and pour over the top of meat and potatoes. Serves 8 to 10.

Variation

Omit the potatoes and serve stew over hot rice.
*Any cut of beef will do—meat gets very tender.

Curried Beef

4 pounds ground beef
6 large onions, diced
3 tablespoons curry powder
2 cups water
8 large ribs of celery, sliced
1 tablespoon Worcestershire sauce
2 tablespoons A-1 Steak Sauce
½ cup catsup
Juice of 1 lemon
1 tablespoon salt (or to taste)
1 tablespoon sugar
2 tablespoons butter or margarine
Mushrooms, if desired

In a large skillet crumble and lightly brown the ground beef. Pour off excess fat. Place beef in a large, heavy pan, such as a Dutch oven or pressure cooker. Put diced onions in skillet with curry powder and water. Cook ten minutes over medium heat. Add onions to meat. Add celery and the rest of the ingredients. Simmer 2 hours or pressure cook at 15 pounds for 10 minutes. (Can be refrigerated or frozen at this point.) Serve over hot rice. Serves 16 to 20. *Note:* Good curry powder is important. We prefer Crosse & Blackwell or Spice Island. This dish seems to improve with age. It can be frozen in family-size containers for use later.

Indian Meat Loaf

4 cups cornflakes
1 pound ground beef
½ pound ground pork
2 eggs, slightly beaten
1 cup cream-style corn
1 cup canned or cooked tomatoes
¼ cup chopped green pepper

1 tablespoon chopped onion
¼ cup chopped parsley
2 teaspoons salt
⅛ teaspoon pepper
½ teaspoon sage
1 teaspoon Worcestershire sauce

Crush cornflakes slightly. Combine with remaining ingredients and mix well. Spread in a greased 9-inch square pan or glass dish. (Can be refrigerated at this point.) Bake at 350° F. about 1 hour. Cut into squares to serve. Serves 8.

Polynesian Meatballs

1 pound ground beef
1 egg
1 teaspoon salt
Pepper to taste
1½ tablespoons finely chopped onion
2 tablespoons flour
1 cup chicken stock
1 tablespoon oil
4 slices pineapple, cut up
3 green peppers, cut into large pieces
3 tablespoons cornstarch
2 teaspoons soy sauce
½ cup vinegar
½ cup sugar

Mix the meat, egg, salt, pepper, and onion. Form into balls; roll in flour and fry in a heavy skillet until light brown. Add ⅓ cup of the chicken stock, oil, pineapple, and green peppers. Simmer over low heat until peppers are tender. Combine remaining ⅔ cup chicken stock, cornstarch, soy sauce, vinegar, and sugar; mix well. Add to meatballs. Heat thoroughly. Serve over rice. Serves 6.

Meatballs and Rice

2 eggs
⅔ cup milk
1 cup soft bread crumbs (about 3 slices of bread)
1 pound ground beef
¼ cup chopped onion
1 teaspoon salt
2 teaspoons baking powder

Pepper to taste
1 can (10 ounces) condensed cream of
**　mushroom soup**
½ soup can of water

In a blender mix the eggs, milk, and bread crumbs. In a large mixing bowl, combine the egg mixture, ground beef, onion, salt, baking powder, and pepper; mix well. Shape into balls and brown in a skillet in a small amount of fat. Transfer to a casserole. Pour off extra fat from skillet. In the remaining drippings heat mushroom soup and water. Pour over meatballs. (Can be refrigerated at this point.) Bake at 350° F. for 40 minutes. Serve over hot rice. Serves 6 to 8. *Note:* The number of servings may be increased by making smaller meatballs and doubling the amount of soup and water.

Swedish Sour Cream Meatballs

Meatballs

2 pounds ground beef
½ cup dry bread crumbs
1 medium onion, chopped
¼ teaspoon pepper
1 teaspoon salt
1 egg
1 teaspoon dry mustard
½ teaspoon paprika
½ teaspoon parsley
½ teaspoon garlic powder

Sauce

1½ cups water flavored with 2 bouillon cubes
1 can (6 ounces) tomato paste
2 teaspoons Worcestershire sauce
2 cups sour cream

Combine the meatball ingredients and form into meatballs. Brown in butter. (Can be refrigerated at this point.) Combine the water-bouillon mixture, tomato paste, and Worcestershire sauce; heat. Add sour cream. Pour over hot meatballs and simmer 10 minutes. Serve over hot noodles. Serves 6 to 8.

Tiny Meatballs

¾ cup dry bread crumbs
1 cup milk
2 pounds ground beef
¼ teaspoon nutmeg
¼ teaspoon allspice
2 eggs
Salt and pepper to taste
1 package dry onion soup mix

Soak bread crumbs in milk until liquid is absorbed. Add remaining ingredients. Mix well and form into tiny meatballs. Arrange in shallow baking pans or on a sheet of foil. Cover and refrigerate or freeze until needed. Bake at 375° F. until brown, about 10 minutes. Serve as a main course or appetizer with Cheese Dip (below) and corn chips. Serves 8 as a main course or 20 as an appetizer.

Cheese Dip

2 pounds Cheddar cheese, grated
1 can (about 4 ounces) green chilies, chopped up
1 package dry onion soup mix
1 can (8 ounces) tomato sauce

Mix all ingredients together in the top of a double boiler. Heat, stirring constantly, until cheese melts.

Variation

Serve meatballs over green noodles or rice.

If we want the perfect host to take us into his eternal home when we come to knock at his door, he has told us himself what we have to do: we must be ready to open our own door to the earthly guests that come our way. (Jean Danielow)

Bitochki

2 cups crumbled fresh bread
1 cup water
2 pounds ground beef
2 teaspoons salt
Dash of pepper
2 onions, minced finely

2 cups sour cream
1 cup dry fine bread crumbs
6 tablespoons butter, melted
2 tablespoons butter
1 cup water
2 cans (10 ounces each) condensed cream of mushroom soup
1 cup milk

Soak bread in 1 cup water. Squeeze out excess liquid. Add the ground beef, salt, pepper, onion, and ¼ cup of the sour cream. Mix well and form into meatballs. Roll in bread crumbs and brown in 6 tablespoons butter. Place in freezer container if for later use, or in a casserole dish. Add 2 tablespoons butter and 1 cup water to drippings in pan and bring to a boil. Add mushroom soup and milk; blend and heat thoroughly. Stir in the rest of the sour cream until blended and pour over meatballs. (Can be refrigerated or frozen at this point.) When ready to serve, bake at 350° F. for 30 to 40 minutes. Serve with rice or noodles. Serves 12.

Beef Noodles Supreme

1 pound lean ground beef*
2 tablespoons butter or margarine
1 clove garlic, chopped or mashed
1 teaspoon salt
1 teaspoon sugar
¼ teaspoon pepper
2 small cans (8 ounces each) tomato sauce
1 package (8 ounces) cream cheese
1 cup sour cream
6 green onions (including green parts), chopped
1 package (8 ounces) noodles
1 cup grated Cheddar cheese

In a skillet, brown beef in butter. Add garlic, salt, sugar, pepper, and tomato sauce; simmer about 10 minutes. Soften and blend thoroughly cream cheese and sour cream. Add onions and set aside. Boil noodles until tender; drain. In a 9" x 13" baking dish, layer noodles, cream cheese mixture, and meat sauce. Repeat layers. Sprinkle cheese on top. (Can be refrigerated at this point.) Bake uncovered at 350° F. for 30 minutes. Serves 8 to 10.

*1 pound sliced frankfurters can be substituted for beef.

Five-Spice Casserole

1 pound ground beef
¾ cup chopped onion
2 cups canned tomatoes
1 can (10 ounces) condensed cream of
    mushroom soup
1½ teaspoons salt
½ bay leaf
⅛ teaspoon each of thyme, oregano,
    garlic powder, and pepper
1 cup instant rice (direct from package)
Grated cheese (as much as you like)

Brown the beef and onion together in a large skillet or Dutch oven. Drain fat. Add tomatoes, soup, and seasonings; blend well. Add rice; cover and simmer for 5 minutes. (Can be refrigerated at this point.) Before serving, sprinkle top with grated cheese and heat just until cheese melts. Serves 6 to 8.

Enchilada Casserole

1 pound lean ground beef
2 tablespoons chili powder
½ cup cooking oil
12 corn tortillas
1½ cans (10 ounces each) enchilada sauce
    diluted with 1 cup water
2 medium onions, finely diced
¾ pound grated Velveeta cheese*
6 medium tomatoes, chopped
Salt and pepper to taste

Brown meat in a heavy skillet; pour off fat. Add chili powder and toss with meat over low heat for 2 to 5 minutes. In a heavy skillet or pan, heat cooking oil to 325° F. Dip tortillas, one at a time, in oil and cook on both sides until soft. Remove with tongs and dip in enchilada sauce. In center of each tortilla, layer meat, onion, cheese, and tomato. Add salt and pepper to taste. Roll up and place seam side down in shallow baking pan. Pour remaining enchilada sauce over the top; sprinkle with remaining meat, onions, and cheese. (Can be refrigerated at this point.) Bake at 300° F. for 30 minutes or until cheese is bubbly.

*Cheese is easier to grate if you put it in freezer 1 hour beforehand.

Tamale Pie

1½ pounds ground beef
½ to 1 cup chopped onions
1 clove garlic, minced
½ cup diced green pepper
1 can (12 ounces) whole kernel corn, drained
2½ cups cooked or canned tomatoes
1½ tablespoons chili powder
1 cup water
½ cup yellow cornmeal
Corn Cheese Topping (below)

Lightly brown meat in a 12-inch skillet. Add onions, garlic, and green pepper. Stir in corn, tomatoes, and chili powder, and simmer for 5 minutes. Mix the water and cornmeal together and stir into meat mixture. Cover and simmer about 8 minutes; then pour into a shallow 3-quart baking dish. (Can be refrigerated at this point.) Top with Corn Cheese Topping. Bake at 375° F. for 30 to 40 minutes. Serves 8 to 10.

Corn Cheese Topping

1½ cups milk
1 teaspoon salt
2 tablespoons butter or margarine
½ cup cornmeal
1 cup (about ¼ pound) shredded sharp Cheddar
    cheese
2 eggs, lightly beaten

Heat together milk, salt, and butter. Slowly stir in cornmeal. Cook until thickened. Remove from heat. Stir in cheese and lightly beaten eggs. Spread over casserole.

Sunday Delight

1 pound ground beef
1 medium Bermuda onion, sliced thin
1 medium potato, sliced thin
1 large tomato, sliced thin
2 carrots, cut in lengthwise strips
Salt and pepper to taste
Worcestershire sauce

Shape ground beef into 6 patties. Place each patty on a 12″ square of aluminum foil. Top each patty with a slice each of onion, potato, tomato, and carrot, salt and pepper to taste, and a dash of Worcestershire sauce. Wrap each stack tightly. (Can be refrigerated at this point.) Make a tiny air hole in top of foil package. Bake at 450° F. for 30 minutes. Serves 6. This is also a good meal for camping: cook the foil-covered patties directly on hot coals for 20 minutes.

Variation

Add a slice of cheese and a dollop of undiluted condensed mushroom soup on top of other ingredients.

Lasagne

1½ to 2 pounds ground beef
1 clove garlic, minced
1 tablespoon parsley flakes
1 tablespoon basil
1½ teaspoons salt
2½ cups cooked or canned tomatoes
2 cans (6 ounces each) tomato paste
6 cups cream-style cottage cheese
2 large eggs, beaten
2 teaspoons salt
½ teaspoon pepper
2 tablespoons parsley flakes
½ cup Parmesan cheese
1 pound Mozzarella cheese, sliced
¼ pound sharp Cheddar cheese, sliced
1 package (10 ounces) lasagne noodles,
**   cooked according to package directions**

In a heavy skillet brown the beef; pour off excess fat. Add garlic, 1 tablespoon parsley flakes, basil, 1½ teaspoons salt, tomatoes, and tomato paste. Simmer, uncovered, until thick, about 45 minutes to 1 hour. Combine the cottage cheese, eggs, 2 teaspoons salt, pepper, 2 tablespoons parsley flakes, and Parmesan cheese. Butter two 13″ x 9″ baking pans. Spread half the noodles on the bottom of pans. Cover with half the cottage cheese mixture, then half the meat sauce, then half the Mozzarella and Cheddar cheese slices. Repeat layers. (Can be refrigerated at this point.) Bake 45 minutes at 375° F. Let stand 10 minutes before serving. Serves 12 generously.

Florentine Lasagne

1 pound link sausage
2 pounds lean ground beef
1 package (10 ounces) lasagne noodles
1 teaspoon salt
2 teaspoons oregano
1 package (10 ounces) frozen chopped spinach,
**   thawed**
2 cans (10 ounces each) condensed cream of
**   mushroom soup**
3 cans (8 ounces each) tomato sauce
1 pound Mozzarella cheese, sliced
1 pound Cheddar cheese, sliced

Slice link sausage and brown in a skillet. Drain off fat and set sausage aside. Crumble and brown ground beef. Combine meats. Cook noodles according to package directions; drain. In a 13″ x 9″ baking pan or dish, make two layers of everything, starting with noodles, then meat and rest of ingredients in order listed, finishing with cheese. (Can be refrigerated at this point.) Bake at 350° F. for 30 minutes or until bubbly. Serves 12.

Beef, Noodles, and Beans Italiano

1 pound lean ground beef
½ pound Italian sausage, crumbled
1 small green pepper, seeded and diced
1½ cups chopped celery, including tops
1 large onion, diced
1½ teaspoons Italian herb seasoning
3 tablespoons chopped parsley
1 tablespoon Worcestershire sauce
1 can (10 ounces) condensed cream of
**   mushroom soup**
1 can (8 ounces) tomato sauce
2 cans (16 ounces each) red kidney beans
**   with liquid**
½ pound fresh mushrooms, sliced
Salt and pepper
Garlic salt

In a skillet, cook the beef and sausage together until brown and crumbly. Pour off excess fat. Add green pepper, celery, and onion; sauté until onion is translucent. Add Italian seasoning, parsley, Worcestershire sauce, soup, to-mato sauce, and beans. Cover and simmer for 20 minutes. (Can be refrigerated at this point. Heat just before serving.) Add mushrooms and cook 1 or 2 minutes. Season to taste with salt, pepper, and garlic salt. Serve over hot cooked noodles. Serves 6.

If every man's care and sorrow
Were written on his brow,
How many would our pity share
Who share our envy now?

Stuffed Cabbage Rolls

1 head cabbage (about 2 pounds)
1 pound ground chuck
½ cup raw rice
2 tablespoons sugar
2 tablespoons minced onion
1 tablespoon lemon juice
2 eggs, beaten slightly
2 tablespoons chili powder (optional)
¼ teaspoon pepper
¼ teaspoon paprika
¼ teaspoon sage
½ teaspoon oregano
¼ teaspoon garlic powder
1 green pepper, seeded and sliced
1 can (16 ounces) tomatoes
1 can (10 ounces) condensed tomato soup
1 bay leaf, crushed
1 teaspoon basil

Wash cabbage; cut out core. Cook whole in boiling water until barely tender. Drain. Combine ground chuck, rice, sugar, onion, lemon juice, eggs, and spices. Separate about 8 large leaves from cabbage. Put a spoonful of meat mixture on each leaf; roll up, tuck in ends, and secure with a toothpick. Place seam down in Dutch oven or roasting pan. Top with green pepper, chopped remaining cabbage, tomatoes, tomato soup, bay leaf, and basil. (Can be frozen or refrigerated at this point.) Cover and bake at 350° F. for 2 hours or until very tender. Serves 8.

Stuffed Zucchini

1 pound lean ground beef
¼ cup butter
1 clove garlic, minced
½ cup finely chopped onion
½ cup diced celery
½ cup soft bread crumbs
1 egg, slightly beaten
1 teaspoon sugar
1 teaspoon salt
Pepper to taste
6 to 8 zucchini, each 6″ long
2 cups canned tomatoes
½ teaspoon basil
Grated cheese

Brown the beef in a skillet; put in mixing bowl and set aside. In the same skillet, melt butter and add garlic, onion, and celery; cook until vegetables are tender. Combine meat, vegetables, crumbs, egg, sugar, salt, and pepper; mix well. Cut a V-shaped strip out of lengthwise side of each zucchini and fill generously with meat mixture. Combine tomatoes and basil and pour into a 9″ x 13″ baking dish. Place stuffed zucchini on top of tomatoes and sprinkle with grated cheese. (Can be refrigerated at this point.) Bake at 350° F. for 35 to 40 minutes. Serves 6 to 8.

Paul Bunyans

¼ pound lean ground beef for each serving
Seasoning salt
Mustard
Pepper or lemon pepper
Dill pickle, thinly sliced
Sweet pickle relish
Bread and butter pickles
Minced onion
Shredded cheese
Sliced mushrooms

For each serving, pat the ¼ pound hamburger into a thin, large patty in the center of a 12-inch square of foil. Sprinkle with seasoning salt and spread with mustard. Cover half of each patty with your choice of any or all of the rest of the ingredients. Fold the patty and the foil in half, making sure that the edges of the patty meet. Press the edges of the patty to seal. Fold the edges of the foil lengthwise several times (drugstore fold) until they touch the edge of the meat. Then fold the ends in the same way in a series of small folds to the edge of the meat. At this point patties may be refrigerated until time to cook.

To Cook Patties

1. Cook in the foil on a buddy burner or tin-can stove, about 5 minutes on each side.
2. Cook over coals at a picnic or outing (you might want to add an extra layer of foil).
3. Bake in an oven at 400° F. for about 15 minutes.
4. Remove foil and broil patties 5 minutes on each side.
5. Remove foil and fry patties on a hot griddle, turning once.
6. Remove foil and cook patties on a barbecue grill about 5 minutes on each side.

Mexican Pile-up

1 large package corn chips
1 pound ground beef
½ cup shredded Cheddar cheese
1 can (30 ounces) refried beans (spicy or plain)
1 bunch green onions, finely sliced
1 small head lettuce, finely shredded
2 medium tomatoes, diced
1 or 2 avocados, sliced (optional)
1 large can (15 ounces) tomato sauce
1 pint sour cream
1 cup sliced olives

In a skillet, brown ground beef. Season to taste. Heat refried beans until bubbly, adding a little water or tomato sauce to thin. Heat the tomato sauce. Serve all other items cold. Place a dish of each item on the table and let each person prepare his own pile-up, starting with the corn chips and adding other items in the order listed, finishing with sour cream and olives. Serves 6 to 8.

LAMB

Alsatian Lamb and Pork Bake

3 tablespoons butter
6 large potatoes, peeled and thinly sliced into salt water
2 large onions, thinly sliced
1 teaspoon salt and pepper to taste
1 to 1½ pounds boneless lamb, thinly sliced
1 to 1½ pounds boneless pork, thinly sliced
½ teaspoon dried thyme leaves or ¼ teaspoon powdered thyme
1 bay leaf
¼ cup chopped fresh parsley
½ cup chicken broth
½ cup white grape juice or apple juice
1 tablespoon cornstarch dissolved in 2 tablespoons water

Butter a large baking dish with 1 tablespoon of the butter. Place half of drained potatoes in dish; cover with half of the onion slices, and season with salt and pepper. Place half of each kind of

meat on onions. Season with salt and pepper and add thyme, bay leaf, and 2 tablespoons of the parsley. Add remaining meat, then onions and potatoes, seasoning all with salt and pepper. Pour juice and broth over. Melt remaining 2 tablespoons of butter and drizzle over potatoes; completely coat the top layer so there will be no discoloration if you plan to prepare on Saturday, refrigerate, and bake on Sunday. Cover and bake 2 hours at 350° F. or 3 hours at 275° to 300° F. Remove cover and add paste of cornstarch and water. Gently shake and tip casserole to blend; return to oven a few minutes to thicken. Brown potatoes under broiler for about 3 minutes. Sprinkle remaining parsley on top. Serves 8 to 10.

Be careful how you live. You may be the only Bible some people read.

Sunday Lamb Stew

2 pounds lamb, cut in 1½-inch cubes
¼ cup flour
1 teaspoon salt
1 teaspoon pepper or to taste
3 tablespoons bacon fat
1 teaspoon minced parsley
½ teaspoon oregano
½ teaspoon sweet basil
2½ cups canned tomatoes
1 cup sliced carrots (1-inch chunks)
3 medium onions, sliced
2 cups diced potatoes (1-inch chunks)
½ cup water

Put flour, salt, and pepper in a paper bag and shake meat in it. Heat fat in a heavy skillet and brown meat well. Stir frequently to brown on all sides. Transfer to a large pot and sprinkle parsley, oregano, and basil. Add tomatoes to pot with meat; cover and simmer 1½ hours. To remaining fat in skillet, add carrots, onions, and potatoes, and sauté lightly a few minutes, just enough to coat with fat and brown slightly. Remove from heat, cover, and let stand. When meat has cooked 1½ hours, add vegetables and stir to blend. Add ½ cup water to skillet and scrape up glaze. Add to pot and simmer another hour or until meat is very tender and vegetables are cooked. (Can be refrigerated at this point.)

If you want gravy a little thicker, stir a little tapioca or cornstarch in a small amount of water to make a paste; add to stew and simmer 5 minutes longer. You may freeze the meat-tomato mixture and add sautéed vegetables later. If you choose to make the stew in two steps, use new bacon fat to brown all vegetables and proceed with recipe. Serves 8 to 10.

Barbecued Leg of Lamb

1 leg of lamb
1 cup Italian or favorite vinegar and oil dressing
1 large clove garlic, minced
⅔ cup finely chopped onion
2 teaspoons barbecue spice
1 teaspoon salt
½ teaspoon oregano
½ teaspoon basil
1 crushed bay leaf

Have butcher bone the leg of lamb and cut it so it will lie fairly flat. (You can do this yourself by holding the leg with the rounded side on the cutting board and, with a small sharp knife, cutting from the large end down to the narrow end. Split open and cut close to bone on both sides until it is free.) Place meat flat in a pan. Prepare a marinade by combining the remaining ingredients; pour over meat. Cover meat and allow to marinate at least overnight, turning once or twice. Broil over hot coals or under a broiler for 45 minutes to 1 hour, turning once and basting several times with marinade. Meat should be slightly pink inside. Serves 6 to 8.

PORK

All-night Pork Bake

1 lean pork roast
1 bottle (16 ounces) barbecue sauce

Place pork roast in roasting pan and bake uncovered at 350° F. for 30 minutes. Add sauce and turn down heat to 220° F. Cover and bake for 8 to 10 hours. Excellent served with pork and beans and coleslaw. Can also be cooked in a slow-cooker pot overnight or all day.

Pork Roast with Sauerkraut

Select a lean pork roast large enough to feed your family. If there is no bone, allow ⅓ to ½ pound per serving. Remove visible fat from roast. Place roast in a baking pan that can be covered tightly. Cover meat with sauerkraut (approximately 1 quart for a 4-pound roast). Cover roasting pan. (Can be refrigerated at this point.) Bake at 275° F. for 5 to 8 hours.

Pork Shoulder Pot Roast

4 pounds boneless pork shoulder roast, tied
2 teaspoons salt
1 teaspoon pepper or to taste
¼ teaspoon thyme
¼ teaspoon oregano
¼ teaspoon fennel (optional)
Flour
2 tablespoons oil, shortening, or rendered pork fat
¾ cup chicken broth
1⅓ cups apple juice or cider
2 cloves garlic, minced
½ teaspoon nutmeg
1 cup sour cream

Combine salt, pepper, thyme, oregano, and fennel, and rub into meat. Dredge meat in flour, rubbing in well. Heat oil in Dutch oven and brown meat on all sides. Add broth, apple juice, garlic, and nutmeg. Cover and simmer on low heat or bake at 250° to 300° F. for 3 hours. Remove meat and make gravy with drippings. Add sour cream and heat but do not boil. Serves 8.

Stuffed Pork Chops Supreme

12 pork chops
1 loaf sourdough or other white bread
1 cup stock or water
3 large onions, diced
6 large ribs celery, diced
½ cup (¼ pound) butter
1 can (10 ounces) condensed cream of mushroom soup
2 teaspoons sage or poultry seasonings
Salt and pepper to taste
Pinch of rosemary and/or basil
Seasoning salt

Prepare dressing: Slice bread and spread on a cookie sheet. Brown in 300° F. oven until very lightly toasted. Cut into small cubes. Moisten bread with stock or water. Sauté onions and celery in butter until tender and translucent. Add bread cubes, soup, sage or poultry seasoning, salt and pepper, rosemary, and basil.

Sprinkle both sides of each chop with seasoning salt. Working on a large piece of heavy aluminum foil, stack chops together with a thick layer of dressing between each. Stand stack on edge with fat side up. Run a skewer through the meat or tie stack with string to hold in place. Bring foil around meat and seal with drugstore-wrap technique. Fold in ends. (Can be refrigerated at this point.) Three hours before serving, place in 300° F. oven. One hour before serving, fold foil down to allow browning. To serve, lift onto platter and remove skewer or string. Garnish platter with cinnamon apple rings. Serves 12.

Variation

Use skinned, boned, and pounded chicken breasts in place of pork chops.

Pork Piquant

8 lean pork chops
½ teaspoon salt
¼ teaspoon pepper
1 can (20 ounces) sliced pineapple
1 cup water
¼ cup vinegar
¼ to ½ cup brown sugar
2 tablespoons lemon juice
1 tablespoon Worcestershire sauce
1 tablespoon prepared mustard
1 teaspoon salt
2 tablespoons cornstarch
1 large can (30 ounces) yams
2 medium onions, thinly sliced and separated into rings
1 teaspoon salt
⅛ teaspoon pepper

Brown pork chops on both sides and arrange in shallow 3-quart casserole. Sprinkle with ½ teaspoon salt and ¼ teaspoon pepper. Drain pineapple and pour juice into a saucepan; reserve slices. To juice, add water, vinegar, brown sugar, lemon juice, Worcestershire sauce, mustard, 1 teaspoon salt, and cornstarch. Cook and stir until thickened. Drain the yams and arrange between the pork chops. Layer onion rings on top of chops and yams. Sprinkle with remaining salt and pepper. Pour sauce over all. (Can be refrigerated overnight at this point.) Cover and bake at 300° F. for 3 hours or bake at 325° F. for 2 hours. Uncover and arrange pineapple over the top; bake uncovered 20 minutes more. Serves 8.

Ham Skillet Dinner

1 fully cooked ham steak, cut ¾ inch thick
    (about 1¼ pounds)
1 tablespoon butter or margarine
1 can (20 ounces) sliced apples, drained
1 can (24 ounces) yams, drained
1 cup pitted dried prunes
½ cup frozen orange juice concentrate, thawed
¼ cup firmly packed brown sugar
¼ teaspoon ground cinnamon
⅛ teaspoon ground cloves

Trim excess fat from ham. Brown ham slowly in melted butter in heavy skillet. Remove to a plate. Arrange drained apple slices in skillet. Place ham on top. Arrange yams and prunes around ham. Combine orange juice concentrate, brown sugar, cinnamon, and cloves; pour over ham slices. Cover and heat over medium heat for 15 minutes. Serves 6.

Ham or Chicken Amandine

¾ cup butter
¾ cup slivered blanched almonds
2 tablespoons minced onion
½ cup plus 1 tablespoon flour
3 cups chicken bouillon
1½ cups heavy cream
4½ cups cooked rice
4 cups cooked ham or chicken
3 tablespoons diced pimiento
2 tablespoons minced parsley
1½ teaspoons salt

Over medium heat, melt butter in a skillet; add almonds and onions, and sauté for 10 minutes. Stir in flour. Add bouillon and cream, and cook, stirring, until thick. Add remaining ingredients. Pour into casserole dish. (Can be refrigerated at this point.) Bake at 350° F. for 30 minutes. Serves 10 to 12.

Torta Prima Vera

Basic Crepe

1½ cups milk
3 eggs
½ teaspoon salt
1 cup flour

Put ingredients in the blender in the order given and blend together at top speed for 30 seconds. Scrape down sides. Blend again. Batter should be the consistency of thick cream. Refrigerate covered for 1 to 2 hours before cooking. Batter thickens on standing. You may need to add a few tablespoons of water.

Before cooking each crepe, brush the crepe pan or skillet with oil. Heat the pan until hot but not smoking. Pour 2 to 3 tablespoons batter into pan; tilt the pan to coat bottom evenly. Cook over medium heat about 1 minute, until top is dry and bottom lightly brown. Tip crepe onto plate. When crepes are cool, stack with wax paper between each crepe.

Torta Filling

½ pound each white and yellow cheese,
    thinly sliced
1 pound cooked chicken or turkey breast,
    thinly sliced
1 pound cooked ham, thinly sliced
6 hard-boiled eggs, sliced
12 large leaves chard or spinach,
    cooked but not cut up
Mayonnaise

On serving plate, layer crepes with cheese slices, meat, and eggs. About every third layer spread a couple of chard leaves over the filling. Continue stacking until the stack is 4 or more inches high. Finish with a crepe. Frost on top with mayonnaise. Decorate just before serving with any or all of the following: pimiento, tomato roses, olives, cream cheese roses, almonds. Keeps well in the refrigerator, well covered, for two days. Cut into wedges to serve. Serves 8.

Kindness is the oil that makes the world run smooth.

Tonnarelli

6 ounces egg noodles
1 cup diced ham (or combination of ham and chicken)
1 can (8 ounces) mushrooms
½ cup chopped onion
½ cup chopped celery
¼ cup butter
¾ cup shredded Cheddar cheese
¼ cup diced bell pepper (optional)
1 can (10 ounces) condensed cream of mushroom soup, undiluted
Pinch of garlic salt
¾ cup Parmesan cheese

Cook the noodles according to package directions. Sauté in butter the ham, mushrooms, onions, and celery. Toss together everything except the Parmesan cheese. Pour into a shallow casserole (about 7″ x 11″) and sprinkle with Parmesan cheese. (Can be refrigerated at this point.) Bake at 350° F. for half an hour or until heated through. Serves 6 to 8.

Pan Quiche

1 loaf white sandwich bread (remove crust and cut slices in half)
1 pound ham, cut into ½-inch cubes
1 pound sharp Cheddar cheese, shredded
6 large eggs
3 cups milk
1 can (10 ounces) condensed cream of mushroom soup
¼ cup finely minced chives

Line a buttered 9″ x 13″ baking dish with half the bread slices to completely cover bottom of dish. Cover with ham pieces, then shredded cheese. Beat the eggs; beat in milk and soup. Pour over ingredients in baking dish. Top with remaining bread slices and sprinkle with ¼ cup finely minced chives. Cover with foil. Refrigerate overnight. Bake covered at 350° F. for 1 hour or until knife inserted in the middle comes out clean. Remove foil for last 10 minutes of cooking. Serves 12 to 15.

Oh the comfort,
The inexpressible comfort,
Of feeling safe with a person,
Having neither to weigh thoughts
Nor measure words,
But pouring them all right out,
Just as they are,
Chaff and grain together,
Certain that a faithful hand
Will take and sift them,
Keep what is worth keeping
and with a breath of kindness
Blow the rest away.
—Dinah Maria Mulock

Sausage and Eggs Continental

4 brown-and-serve sausages
6 tablespoons butter or margarine
2 small onions, thinly sliced
1 medium-size green pepper, thinly sliced
½ teaspoon garlic salt
¼ teaspoon crushed thyme
⅛ teaspoon pepper
3 cups loosely packed frozen hash brown potatoes
8 eggs
½ teaspoon salt
2 small tomatoes, cut in thin wedges

Slice the sausages thin. Brown lightly in a large skillet; remove with a slotted spoon into a bowl. Add 2 tablespoons of the butter to drippings. Stir in onion and green pepper and sauté until tender-crisp. Stir in garlic salt, thyme, and pepper. Spoon mixture into bowl with sausages. Add another 2 tablespoons butter to the skillet; stir in potatoes. Cover; cook 5 minutes. Add remaining 2 tablespoons butter to the skillet. Beat eggs with the salt till frothy and pour over potatoes in the pan. Cover and cook slowly until eggs are set.

Spoon onion-sausage mixture over the eggs; continue cooking, covered, to heat sausage. Place tomato wedges on top. Cover and heat 1 minute more. Cut in wedges to serve. Serves 4.

POULTRY

very good

Chicken Adobo

1 whole chicken
⅔ cup apple cider vinegar
1 cup soy sauce
3 or 4 small garlic cloves
3 or 4 large onions, sliced

Squeeze chicken into a pan that is deep enough so that it is covered but small enough around so that a minimum amount of water is needed to cover chicken. Add vinegar, soy sauce, and garlic, and enough water to barely cover chicken. Cover chicken with sliced onions. Cover and bring to a boil. Lower heat to simmer. Chicken will be cooked in about an hour, but it may be simmered for up to two hours, if you need to be away longer. Remove to a platter and surround with hot rice. If desired, serve chicken stock over rice. Serves 4 to 6.

Refrigerate remaining stock for use in soup or to cook bulgur or rice in. Or hard-boiled eggs may be peeled and marinated in the stock.

Thankful hearts are earthly dwelling places of God.

Garlic Fried Chicken

1 frying chicken, cut up
1 cup sour cream
1 teaspoon Worcestershire sauce
1 tablespoon lemon juice
2 cloves garlic, mashed
½ teaspoon salt
½ teaspoon paprika
½ teaspoon celery salt

On the day before serving, place chicken in a bowl. Combine remaining ingredients and pour over chicken, making sure all pieces are coated. Cover and let stand in refrigerator overnight. Drain chicken pieces, dredge in flour, and fry in half an inch of hot fat until chicken is tender and has a light brown crust, about 40 to 50 minutes. Serves 6.

Quick Yummy Chicken

1 cup raw rice
1 cup water
1 chicken, cut into pieces
⅔ package onion soup mix
2 cans (10 ounces each) condensed cream of mushroom soup
1 soup can water

Swish rice and water around in a 9″ x 13″ baking dish. Lay chicken pieces on top and sprinkle with onion soup mix. Blend mushroom soup and water and pour over chicken. Cover with foil. Bake at 350° F. for 1 hour, or at 300° F. for 2 hours, or at 250° F. for 3 hours. Remove foil for last half hour of baking time. Serves 6.

Barbecued Chicken

3 pounds of chicken pieces
⅔ cup flour
Garlic salt to taste
Pepper to taste
1 medium onion, chopped
2 tablespoons fat or oil
2 tablespoons wine vinegar
2 tablespoons brown sugar
¼ cup lemon juice
1 cup catsup
3 tablespoons Worcestershire sauce
½ tablespoon prepared mustard
1 cup chopped celery
1 cup chopped green pepper (optional)
½ cup (¼ pound) butter

In a paper bag, combine flour with garlic salt and pepper. Add chicken pieces, 2 or 3 at a time, and shake to coat; set aside. Sauté onion in fat or oil until onion is clear; add vinegar, brown sugar, lemon juice, catsup, Worcestershire sauce, mustard, celery, and green peppers. In a heavy skillet, melt butter and brown chicken pieces. Arrange chicken in a casserole dish. Pour sauce over chicken. (Can be refrigerated at this point.) Bake at 325° F. for 1 hour. Serve over hot rice. Serves 8.

Portuguese Chicken

1 large frying chicken (3 pounds or more)
2 tablespoons minced garlic
2 tablespoons dried parsley
2 tablespoons oregano
½ cup cooking oil
2 tablespoons salt
Pepper to taste

Wash whole chicken and dry well inside and out with paper towels. In mortar and pestle or blender, mix all spices and cooking oil. Smear oil mixture over chicken, inside and out. Bake at 400° F. for 1 hour, basting frequently. Serve over rice (wild rice for special occasions). Serves 6. *Note:* This is also a delicious way to prepare a small turkey.

Orange-glazed Chicken

6 to 8 chicken breast halves,
**   or 1 whole chicken, cut in pieces**
½ cup Italian salad dressing
½ small can (6 ounces) frozen orange juice
**   concentrate, thawed**
½ cup orange marmalade

Remove skin from chicken and place chicken pieces in a single layer in a baking dish. Pour dressing over chicken, making sure it is coated on all sides. Use a little more than ½ cup, if needed. Cover and let stand overnight in the refrigerator. About an hour before serving, pour off any excess dressing. Brush chicken with a mixture of the orange concentrate and marmalade and bake uncovered at 325° F. for about 1 hour. Baste frequently. Serves 6 to 8.

Elegant Stuffed Chicken

8 chicken breast halves
6 tablespoons butter
3 medium zucchini (about 1½ pounds),
**   shredded coarsely**
5 slices sourdough or other white bread
2 medium eggs, slightly beaten
1 cup (3 to 4 ounces) shredded Swiss cheese
¼ teaspoon pepper

1 teaspoon salt (or to taste)
Melted butter
Lemon pepper

Skin and bone the chicken breasts. Pound each breast until thin (do not tear flesh). Set aside. In a 3-quart skillet or saucepan, melt 6 tablespoons butter; add zucchini and cook, stirring, for 2 minutes. Remove from heat. Tear bread into small pieces and stir into zucchini. Add eggs, cheese, pepper, and salt. (If you plan to store for a day before serving, cool the dressing in the refrigerator before stuffing the chicken breasts.) Fill each breast with a large scoop of dressing; fold over and arrange in a shallow baking dish. (Can be covered and stored in refrigerator at this point.) Brush the tops of chicken breasts with melted butter and sprinkle with lemon pepper. Bake at 400° F. for 45 to 50 minutes. Serves 8.

Chicken Macadamia

2 tablespoons butter
1 jar (3½ ounces) macadamia nuts
**   (no substitutions)**
2 eggs
¼ cup peanut oil or other salad oil
2 tablespoons soy sauce
1 tablespoon minced ginger root
**   or 1 teaspoon powdered ginger**
¼ teaspoon pepper
2 tablespoons white grape juice or water
1 medium onion, minced
¼ cup cold water
½ cup flour
¼ cup cornstarch
6 chicken breast halves

Melt butter in shallow pan in oven heated to 350° F. Add nuts and toast in oven, stirring frequently, until light brown (about 15 minutes). Avoid scorching. In blender, blend well the eggs, peanut oil, soy sauce, ginger, pepper, grape juice, onion, cold water, flour, and cornstarch to make batter. Skin and bone chicken breasts. Slice the chicken across the grain into thin pieces; scrape little pieces off the bone also. Soak the chicken pieces in the batter for 30 minutes (or overnight in the refrigerator, if desired). In an electric skillet or wok, heat ¼ cup peanut oil to 350° F. Stir-fry chicken in oil until medium brown on both sides. Remove to platter and sprinkle with macadamia nuts. Serve over hot rice. Serves 6.

Chicken and Dried Beef Casserole

1 package (3½ ounces) or 1 small jar dried beef
6 chicken breast halves, boned and skinned
3 lean strips bacon, cut in half
1 can (10 ounces) condensed cream of
   mushroom soup
1 cup sour cream
½ cup sliced fresh mushrooms
   or 1 can (6 ounces) mushrooms, drained

Tear beef in pieces and spread in a shallow baking dish. Place chicken breasts on top of beef and place ½ slice of bacon on each piece. Combine soup, sour cream, and mushrooms, and pour over chicken. (Can be refrigerated at this point.) Bake, covered, at 300° F. for 1½ hours. Uncover and bake 30 minutes longer. Serves 6.

Allison recommends

Chicken Mincemeat

Chicken pieces for 6 to 8 persons
¼ cup shortening, butter, oil, or margarine
1 clove garlic, minced
Salt and pepper to taste
1 packet (9 ounces) dehydrated mincemeat
2 cups water
2 cups chopped onions
1 teaspoon curry powder
Grated rind and juice of 1 lemon
2 teaspoons vinegar

Heat shortening or oil in a heavy skillet; brown garlic. Add chicken pieces; brown. Season with salt and pepper. Place chicken pieces in a large casserole. Crumble mincemeat in a saucepan. Add water and cook, stirring, until lumps disappear; boil 1 minute. Add onions, curry powder, lemon rind and juice, and vinegar; blend well. Pour over chicken. Cover casserole. (Can be refrigerated at this point.) Bake at 350° F. for 1 hour or 250° F. for 3 hours. Serves 6 to 8.

Lemon Chicken

Chicken pieces for 6 to 8 persons
¼ cup shortening, butter, oil, or combination
2 cups chopped onions
½ pound mushrooms, sliced
¼ cup flour
1 teaspoon dry mustard
1 teaspoon dried basil
1 teaspoon salt
Pepper to taste
1 cup light cream or canned milk, scalded
1½ cups chicken broth
⅓ cup lemon juice
Grated rind of 2 lemons
½ cup sour cream (optional)

In a heavy skillet, brown chicken in fat. Remove to a large casserole. Add onions and mushrooms to remaining fat and cook until onions are translucent. Stir in flour and seasonings and blend. Combine cream and broth and add; cook until thickened. Stir in lemon juice and rind, and pour over chicken in casserole. Cover. (Can be refrigerated at this point.) Bake at 350° F. for 1 hour or at 250° F. for 3 hours. Just before serving, stir in sour cream, if desired. Serves 6 to 8.

Florentine Chicken

Chicken pieces for 6 to 8 persons
½ cup flour
1½ teaspoons salt
Pepper to taste
¼ cup shortening, oil, butter, or combination
1½ teaspoons salt
2 cups sour cream
½ cup heavy cream
¼ cup apple juice or white grape juice
1 medium onion, coarsely chopped
1 clove garlic (or more, if desired)
1 tablespoon lemon juice
2 packages (10 ounces each) fresh spinach,
   washed and well drained*

Combine flour, salt, and pepper in paper bag and shake chicken pieces in it, a few at a time. Set aside remaining flour. In a heavy skillet, heat fat and brown chicken pieces. Remove from pan, reserving pan juices. Place sour cream, cream, apple juice, onion, garlic, lemon juice, and the reserved flour in a blender and blend on low until smooth—about 10 seconds. Pour over the spinach and toss until all is coated. Pile spinach in a 5- or 6-quart casserole. Place chicken on top, pour reserved pan juices over all, and cover. (Can be refrigerated at this point.) Bake at 350° F. for 1 hour or at 225° F. for 3 hours. Serves 6 to 8.

*This amount makes very large servings of spinach. You may wish to use only 1 to 1½ packages, but it is delicious reheated.

Chicken Chow Mein

¼ cup oil, chicken fat, or butter
4 cups celery, sliced thin diagonally
2 cups green pepper, sliced thin
2 cups fresh mushrooms, sliced or whole
    (may also use canned or dried)
2 cups chicken stock or water
3 cups cooked chicken or turkey,
    cut into bite-sized pieces
¼ cup cornstarch
½ cup water
½ cup soy sauce
1 cup chopped pimiento
Chow mein noodles
1 cup toasted slivered almonds

Heat oil in a large wok or skillet. Add celery, peppers, and mushrooms, and stir fry over high heat just until slightly tender. Add stock or water and chicken and bring to a boil. Blend cornstarch and water and add to hot mixture. Stir in soy sauce and pimiento. Serve immediately over Chinese fried noodles. Let each person top his chow mein with the almonds. Serves 12.

Note: This is an excellent dish for parties as well as for Sunday. Prepare all ingredients the day before and refrigerate. Since it takes only 10 minutes to cook, it can be started when guests arrive.

God, give us serenity to accept what cannot be changed, courage to change what should be changed, and the wisdom to distinguish the one from the other. (Reinhold Neinbuhr)

Chicken Olé

8 chicken breast halves
1 dozen corn tortillas
1 can (10 ounces) condensed cream of
    chicken soup
1 can (10 ounces) condensed cream of
    mushroom soup
1 cup milk
1 onion, grated
2 cans (7 ounces each) green chilies, chopped
1 cup grated Cheddar cheese

Wrap chicken breasts in foil and bake at 300° F. for 1 hour. Reserve broth from foil. Cool chicken breasts; then skin and bone chicken and cut in large pieces. Tear tortillas in 1" squares or strips. Combine soups, milk, onion, and chilies. Butter a large, shallow baking dish. Put 2 to 3 tablespoons of reserved chicken broth in bottom of dish. Place a layer of tortilla pieces in dish, then a layer of chicken, and spoon over soup mixture. Repeat layers two or three times, ending with soup mixture. Top with cheese. Refrigerate for 24 hours. Bake at 300° F. for 1 to 1½ hours. Serves 6 to 8.

Almond Chicken Rice Bake

1 cup raw Minute Rice, cooked as directed
    on package
2 to 3 cups cooked chicken, cut up
2 cans (10 ounces each) condensed cream of
    chicken soup
1 tablespoon lemon juice
1 cup mayonnaise or salad dressing
1 cup chopped celery
1 tablespoon minced onion
3 tablespoons butter
½ cup slivered almonds
½ cup crushed cornflakes

Place cooked rice in greased 9" x 13" baking dish; cover with chicken. Blend soup, lemon juice, mayonnaise, celery, and onion, and pour over chicken. Melt butter and stir in almonds and cornflakes. Sprinkle on top of casserole. (Can be covered and refrigerated at this point. Remove from refrigerator at least 2 hours before baking.) Bake uncovered at 300° F. for 1 hour. Serves 8 to 10.

Dinner's in the Oven

½ cup (¼ pound) margarine
1 chicken, cut into 8 pieces
Salt, pepper, and paprika to taste
1 package (10 ounces) frozen peas, thawed
1 can (16 ounces) whole onions, well drained
1 can (10 ounces) condensed cream of
    mushroom soup
3 tablespoons grape juice (optional)
3 large potatoes
1 cup cornflake crumbs

Melt margarine in a large skillet over medium heat. Set aside ¼ cup. Sprinkle chicken with salt, pepper, and paprika. Brown chicken in margarine. Drain on paper towels. Place chicken in a 3-quart casserole dish. Add peas and onions. Mix soup with grape juice; pour over chicken. Cover. (Can be refrigerated at this point.) Wash and scrub potatoes; cut into ½-inch slices. Dip into reserved melted margarine; coat with crumbs and sprinkle with salt. Place on ungreased baking sheet. Put both casserole and potatoes in oven heated to 350° F. Bake 1 hour. Serves 6 to 8.

Sausage-stuffed Chicken Roll

6 chicken breast halves
1 pound link or Italian-style sausage
½ cup water
1 cup fresh bread crumbs
2 eggs
Seasoning salt
Lemon pepper
¾ pound thick-sliced bacon

Skin and bone the chicken breasts; cut each in half and pound until flat and even in thickness. Set aside. In a 10-inch skillet, heat sausages and water to boiling; cover and simmer for 5 minutes. Remove cover and continue cooking, stirring frequently, until well browned. Remove to paper towel and finely chop. Pour off any grease remaining in skillet (reserve grease). In the skillet combine the bread crumbs, eggs, and sausage, stirring to combine with brown bits from the pan.

Arrange flattened chicken breasts on a sheet of foil 4 across and 2 on the ends, overlapping slightly to make a rectangle about 10" x 12". Sprinkle with seasoning salt and lemon pepper. Spread sausage dressing over the chicken evenly, not quite to the edges.

Lay a long skewer lengthwise over the meat and dressing. Picking up the far edge of the foil, gently roll the meat toward you, jelly-roll-fashion, until it is all rolled and dressing is covered, with the skewer inside the roll. Lay bacon strips, edges touching, on foil from chicken roll to far edge of foil. Lift the edge of foil closest to you and gently let the meat roll over onto the bacon. Pick up the bacon ends and bring bacon around the meat; secure with toothpicks until all the meat is closely covered with the bacon. Holding both ends of the skewer, lift roll off the foil and place in a baking pan. (Can be refrigerated at this point.) Bake at 350° F. for 1½ hours. Serve hot on a bed of rice. If desired, make a gravy using the pan drippings. Serves 8 to 10.

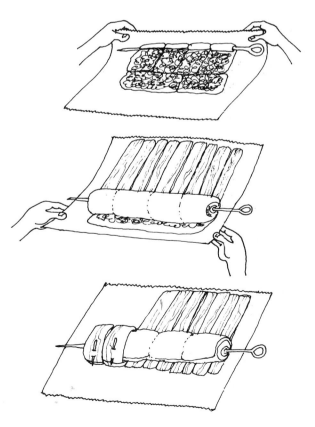

Hot Chicken Salad

2 cups cooked chicken, skinned, boned,
    and cut in bite-size pieces
1 cup diced celery
1 tablespoon minced onion
½ cup coarsely chopped pecans or almonds
3 hard-boiled eggs, sliced thin
1 can (10 ounces) condensed cream of chicken
    soup or 1 cup medium white sauce
½ teaspoon salt
¼ teaspoon black pepper
1 tablespoon lemon juice
¾ cup mayonnaise
2 cups crushed potato chips
    or buttered bread crumbs

Fold together all ingredients except potato chips. Spoon into a baking dish and cover with foil. (Can be refrigerated at this point.) Bake, covered, at 350° F. for 30 minutes or until bubbly and hot. Remove foil and sprinkle chicken with potato chips. Bake uncovered a few minutes longer. Serves 8.

Chicken Logs

8 chicken breast halves, skinned,
    boned, and pounded
Salt and pepper to taste
1 tablespoon Dijon mustard
½ cup (about 2 ounces) crumbled Roquefort
    or blue cheese
½ cup shredded Swiss cheese
2 tablespoons butter, softened
1 egg, slightly beaten
1 cup flour
2 cups soft bread crumbs
¼ cup butter

Salt and pepper each chicken breast and spread with a thin layer of mustard. Blend the cheeses and 2 tablespoons butter with a fork. Divide into eight equal parts and form into rolls. Place a roll lengthwise on each chicken breast; then roll and fold each breast to enclose the cheese. Roll the chicken in flour to coat; dip into egg, then in bread crumbs. Place chicken breast seam down in a flat baking pan. (At this point dish may be covered tightly with foil and refrigerated.) Heat ¼ cup butter in a small, heavy skillet. Cook the chicken rolls 2 or 3 at a time, turning until golden brown. Return to baking pan. Heat oven to 350° F. Place in oven and bake for 12 to 15 minutes. (If preferred, the browning step may be omitted and the rolls placed in the oven for 35 to 40 minutes.) Serves 8.

Variation

Instead of the cheese sticks, prepare a seasoned butter stick: Combine with a fork ¾ cup butter or margarine, 1 small minced clove of garlic, 1 teaspoon rosemary, 1 teaspoon marjoram, and 1 tablespoon soy sauce. Spread on a small rectangle of foil and refrigerate until butter is set. Cut into 8 strips, each ½-inch wide. Place each stick on a chicken breast and proceed as above.

Be at war with your vices, at peace with your neighbors, and let every New Year find you a better man. (Benjamin Franklin)

Jalapeño Chicken Enchiladas

2 cups chopped cooked chicken
1 package (8 ounces) cream cheese, softened
½ cup chopped onion
½ teaspoon salt
8 corn tortillas
Cooking oil
1 pound Jalapeño pepper Velveeta cheese,
    cubed
2 cups chopped tomatoes
¼ cup milk

Heat oven to 350° F. Combine chicken, cream cheese, onion, and salt. Fry tortillas in ¼-inch-deep oil until just pliable. Fill tortillas with chicken mixture. Roll and place seam side down in a baking dish. Heat Velveeta cheese, 1 cup of the tomatoes, and milk over low heat, stirring until cheese is melted. Pour over tortillas. Place remaining tomatoes on top. (Can be covered with foil and refrigerated at this point.) Bake uncovered at 350° F. for 30 minutes. Serves 8.

Chicken Tamale Pie

- 1 large chicken (about 3½ to 4 pounds)
- 2 large onions, chopped
- ½ cup butter
- ¼ cup flour
- 2½ cups canned or fresh chopped tomatoes
- ¾ cup pitted ripe olives
- 1½ teaspoons salt
- 1½ teaspoons chili powder
- 1 teaspoon pepper

Simmer chicken in water until tender. Remove skin and bones and cut chicken in large pieces. In a large skillet, sauté onions in butter until tender, about ten minutes. Stir in the flour. Add the rest of the ingredients except the chicken and cook until slightly thickened. Arrange chicken in a buttered 9" x 13" glass baking dish. Cover with the sauce and cool. (Can be refrigerated at this point.) One hour before serving time cover chicken with batter (below) and bake at 350° F. for 1 hour. Serves 8 to 10.

Tamale Batter

- 1 cup flour
- 1 cup yellow cornmeal
- 1 cup melted butter
- 2 teaspoons baking powder
- 1 teaspoon salt
- 2½ cups milk

Mix all ingredients together and pour over chicken. Batter may be mixed in a blender (put milk in first). Batter will be thin.

Turkey Barbecue

- 3 to 4 pounds turkey breast,
  sliced 1 to 1½ inches thick
  (allow ¼ to ½ pound per person)
- 2 cups carbonated lemon-lime beverage
- 1 cup soy sauce
- 1 cup cooking oil
- ¼ teaspoon garlic powder
- ½ teaspoon horseradish

Marinate the turkey slices in a sauce made of all the other ingredients for at least 3 hours or over-night. Remove from the marinade and cook over hot coals to the desired doneness. Depending on thickness, it takes 5 to 10 minutes on each side. The turkey breasts may also be cooked whole and then sliced for serving. It takes about 45 minutes to cook whole breast on a covered grill. Cut-up chicken pieces are also delicious prepared this way.

Turkey Tetrazzini

- ¼ cup butter
- ¼ cup flour
- 1 teaspoon salt
- ¼ teaspoon nutmeg
- 2 cups turkey broth
- 1 cup light cream
- ¼ cup white grape juice (optional)
- ¼ cup grated Parmesan cheese
- ¼ cup grated Gruyère cheese
  (or any white cheese)
- 1 egg yolk
- 3 cups cooked turkey, cubed
- 1 pound sliced mushrooms
- 8 ounces spaghetti
- ½ cup slivered almonds

Melt butter over low heat; blend in flour, salt, and nutmeg and cook, stirring constantly, until mixture is smooth and bubbly. Remove from heat. Stir in broth and cream, then bring to boil and cook, stirring, 1 minute. Stir in grape juice and cheeses. Stir a little of the hot mixture into egg yolk and return to sauce. Blend thoroughly. Add mushrooms and turkey. (Can be refrigerated at this point.)

Preheat oven to 350° F. Break spaghetti into 2-inch pieces and drop into 6 cups rapidly boiling salted water. Bring again to boil. Stir constantly with wooden spoon or fork for 3 minutes. Cover and remove from heat. Let stand for 10 minutes, then drain in colander. Place spaghetti in buttered baking dish and pour turkey and sauce over spaghetti and sprinkle with almonds. Bake uncovered at 325° F. for 25 to 30 minutes. Let stand for 10 minutes before serving. Serves 8 to 10.

SEAFOOD

Crab and Shrimp Casserole

¼ cup butter or margarine
¼ cup flour
2 cups milk
1 can (about 6 ounces) crabmeat, drained
1 can (about 6 ounces) shrimp, rinsed and deveined, if necessary
1 cup frozen peas, defrosted
½ cup blanched almonds, slivered
½ cup stuffed olives, sliced
1 cup cooked small-size macaroni
½ teaspoon salt
¼ teaspoon pepper
1 teaspoon dry mustard
1 egg white
1 cup salad dressing or mayonnaise

Melt butter in saucepan; add flour and blend. Add milk and blend well. Cook, stirring constantly, until sauce is thick and smooth. Remove from heat. To white sauce add crabmeat, shrimp, peas, almonds, olives, macaroni, and seasonings. Pour into 1½-quart casserole. Beat egg white until stiff. Fold in salad dressing and spread over casserole. Bake at 350° F. for 30 minutes. Makes 8 to 10 servings. For special occasions, bake in individual clam shells, topped with a dollop of the egg-white and salad dressing topping.

Crab Diablo

3 tablespoons butter
2 tablespoons finely chopped onion
3 tablespoons flour
1 teaspoon dry mustard
¾ teaspoon salt
Dash of pepper
½ teaspoon paprika
1 teaspoon Worcestershire sauce
1 cup milk
½ cup half-and-half
2 cups or 2 cans (6 ounces each) crabmeat*
½ cup buttered crumbs

½ cup grated Cheddar cheese
Parmesan cheese
Paprika

Heat butter in a saucepan and add onion. Cook over low heat until onion is soft but not browned. Blend in flour, seasonings, and Worcestershire sauce. Slowly add milk and cook, stirring constantly, over low heat until thickened. Blend in half-and-half. Add crab. Fill buttered shells or casserole dish with crab mixture. Sprinkle with crumbs, cheeses, and paprika. (Can be refrigerated at this point.) Bake at 350° F. for 20 to 25 minutes or until browned. Serves 6 to 8.

*Artificial crabmeat is delicious prepared this way.

There is no lonelier person than the one who lives with a spouse with whom he or she cannot communicate. (Margaret Mead)

Seafood Casserole

¼ cup butter
¼ cup flour
2 cups milk
Salt and pepper to taste
Dash of nutmeg
2 cups sharp Cheddar cheese, grated
1 small can diced pimiento
1 can (6 ounces) crabmeat
1 can (4½ ounces) shrimp, drained (or tuna, if desired)
1 can (16 ounces) cream-style corn

In a saucepan melt butter; add flour and stir over low heat until well blended but not browned. Add milk and seasonings and cook, stirring, until thick. Add cheese and stir until melted. Carefully stir in remaining ingredients and pour into a greased 9-inch square baking dish. (Can be refrigerated at this point.) Bake at 325° F. for 1 hour. Serves 8.

Seafood Lasagne

10 lasagne noodles
2 tablespoons butter or margarine
1 cup chopped onion
1 package (8 ounces) cream cheese
1½ cups cottage cheese
2 eggs, beaten
1 teaspoon basil, crushed
¼ teaspoon oregano, crushed
2 tablespoons parsley, chopped
½ teaspoon salt
Pepper to taste
1 can (6 ounces) crabmeat, drained
**1 can (4½ ounces) shrimp, rinsed and
    deveined if necessary**
**2 cans (10 ounces each) condensed cream of
    mushroom soup**
½ cup milk
2 tablespoons lemon juice
½ cup Parmesan cheese

Cook noodles according to directions on package; drain. Arrange half of the noodles in the bottom of a 9″ x 13″ greased baking dish. Sauté onion in butter until tender. Blend in cream cheese. Stir in cottage cheese, eggs, basil, oregano, and parsley; add salt and pepper to taste. Spread half on top of noodles. Combine

---

I don't know what your destiny will be, but one thing I know: the only ones among you who will be really happy are those who have sought and found how to serve. (Albert Schweitzer)

---

soup, milk, and lemon juice. Gently stir in crabmeat and shrimp. Spread half over cheese layer. Repeat these three layers. Sprinkle Parmesan cheese over all. (Can be refrigerated, if desired.) Bake at 350° F. for 45 minutes. Let stand 15 minutes before serving. Serves 12 to 15.

Crab Casserole

2 cups or 2 cans (6 ounces each) crabmeat
2 cups half-and-half
**2 cups mayonnaise or salad dressing
    (or combination)**
**4 slices white bread, cut in small cubes
    (cut off crusts)**
12 hard-boiled eggs, cubed
1 tablespoon chopped parsley
1 tablespoon chopped onion
2 teaspoons salt
⅓ cup crushed cornflakes

Stir together all ingredients except cornflakes, and pour into a 9″ x 13″ baking dish. Cover with crushed cornflakes. (Can be refrigerated at this point.) Bake at 350° F. for 30 minutes (35 to 40 minutes if refrigerated). Serves 10 to 12.

That house which is not often swept makes the queenly inhabitant soon loath it; and that heart which is not continually purifying itself is not a fit place for the Spirit of God to dwell in. (Anne Bradstreet)

By their fruits ye shall know them

Salads, Vegetables, Pasta, and Egg Dishes

Salads

Overnight Tossed Green Salad	29
Hapsburg Cucumbers	29
Cucumber Gelatin Salad	29
Japanese Cucumber Salad	29
Yogurt and Cucumber Salad	29
Fire and Ice Salad	30
Frozen Cole Slaw	30
Sweet and Snappy Cole Slaw	30
Cauliflower Slaw	30
24-Hour Cabbage Salad	30
Pickled Beets and Eggs	31
Green Bean Potato Dill Salad	31
Chicken Won Ton Salad	31
Taco Salad Extraordinaire	32
Frozen Cranberry Salad	32
Instant Fruit Salad	32
Lime Wreath Mold	32
Minted Fruit and Vegetable Salad	33
Favorite Standby Frozen Salad	33
Artichoke and Rice Salad	33
Berry-Cheese Salad	33

Salad Dressings

Thousand Island Dressing	34
Blue Cheese Dressing	34
Honey Lemon Dressing	34
Lemon Fruit Dressing	34
Raspberry Creme Dressing	34

Vegetables

Rotkohl (German Red Cabbage)	35
Scalloped Cabbage	35
Creamed Cauliflower and Peas	
Ratatouille	35
Carrots Sweet and Sour	36
Vegetable Medley	36
Garden Medley	36
Green Spinach Croustade	36
Spinach Pudding	37
Broccoli-Cheese Casserole	37
Broccoli-Cheese Scallop	37
Carrot and Cabbage Casserole	37
Cauliflower with Almonds	38
Summer Special	38
Baked Beans	38
Sour Cream Potato Casserole	38
Fast Cheesy Potatoes	38
Cream-Cheesy Potatoes	38
Pan-fried Potatoes	39
Potato Pancakes	39
Yum-Yum Potatoes	39
Easy Pilaf	39
Noodles and Nuts	40
Salsa Verde Pasta	40
Spanish Tortilla	40
Basic Rice Luncheon Dish	40
Golden Mushroom Puff	41
Cheese Puff	41
Chili Relleno Casserole	41

SALADS

Overnight Tossed Green Salad

1 head lettuce, torn in pieces
1 purple onion, chopped, or
   1 cup sliced green onions
1 cup chopped celery
1 package (10 ounces) frozen peas (not thawed)
½ green pepper, chopped
1 can (about 5 ounces) water chestnuts,
   drained and sliced
4 hard-boiled eggs, sliced
½ pound bacon, fried crisp and crumbled
   (optional)
2 cups mayonnaise
4 ounces Cheddar cheese, shredded

Layer everything except mayonnaise and cheese in order given in a salad bowl (salad looks pretty in a glass bowl). Spread mayonnaise over top, sealing to edge. Sprinkle with cheese. Refrigerate overnight. Serves 8 to 10.

Hapsburg Cucumbers

3 medium cucumbers, sliced very thin
1 large mild onion, sliced very thin
Salt
Vinegar
Oil
1 cup sour cream
Dash of pepper
Parsley
Paprika

In a bowl alternate layers of cucumber and onion. Sprinkle each layer heavily with salt. Barely cover with ice water; cover bowl and refrigerate for several hours. Drain cucumbers and onions in a strainer; wash quickly in running water; then drain again. Place in a bowl, and cover with equal parts of vinegar and oil. Cover bowl and marinate salad several hours or overnight. Just before serving, drain off marinade and stir in sour cream and pepper. Garnish with parsley and paprika. Serves 6.

Cucumber Gelatin Salad

1 cucumber
1 medium onion
1 small package (3 ounces) lime-flavored gelatin
¾ cup boiling water
1 carton (16 ounces) cottage cheese, drained
1 cup mayonnaise

Grind the cucumber and onion (or chop in food processor). Dissolve gelatin in boiling water. Cool. Add cottage cheese, mayonnaise, and ground cucumber and onions. Stir together and refrigerate until firm. Serves 6 to 8.

Japanese Cucumber Salad

2 large cucumbers
⅓ cup white vinegar
4 teaspoons sugar
1 teaspoon salt
Dash of monosodium glutamate

Cut cucumbers in half lengthwise and remove any large seeds. Slice crosswise into very thin slices. Sprinkle about a teaspoon of salt over slices, and after a minute or two squeeze the water out of the cucumber. Marinate at least 12 hours in refrigerator in a mixture of the vinegar, sugar, salt, and monosodium glutamate. Serves 4 to 6.

Yogurt and Cucumber Salad

1 clove garlic
Salt and pepper
2 or 3 medium cucumbers, peeled
6 or 7 fresh mint leaves
2 cartons (6 ounces each) plain yogurt

Crush garlic clove in bottom of salad bowl and rub around bowl. Remove pulp. Sprinkle salt and pepper in bottom of bowl and rub together. Cut cucumbers in quarters lengthwise, then in bite-size pieces. Place in salad bowl and stir to blend well with salt, pepper, and garlic. Remove stems from mint leaves. Chop leaves finely and stir into cucumbers. Stir in yogurt. Refrigerate until ready to serve. Serves 6 to 8.

Fire and Ice Salad

6 large ripe tomatoes, peeled and cut in wedges
1 red onion, thinly sliced
1 green pepper, thinly sliced
¼ teaspoon salt
¼ cup sugar
¾ cup vinegar
⅛ teaspoon cayenne (optional)
¼ cup water
1½ teaspoons mustard seed
1 avocado, cut in wedges
1 large cucumber, peeled and sliced

Place tomatoes, onions, and green peppers in bowl. Combine salt, sugar, vinegar, cayenne, water, and mustard seed and bring to a boil. Cool. Pour over vegetables and refrigerate overnight. Just before serving, add avocado wedges and cucumbers. Serves 8.

Frozen Cole Slaw

1 medium cabbage
1 cup vinegar
¼ cup water
1 teaspoon salt
1 cup sugar
1 teaspoon mustard seed
1 teaspoon celery seed

Shred the cabbage. Cover with cold water; add 1 teaspoon salt, and let stand for 1 hour. Meanwhile, make syrup by bringing to a boil the rest of the ingredients and cooking one minute. Let stand until lukewarm. Drain cabbage well. Pour syrup over cabbage and mix well. Put into a covered container and refrigerate or freeze. When ready to serve, thaw and use "as is" or, for variety, add ⅓ cup mayonnaise, shredded carrot, and raisins. Serves 6 to 8.

Note: This is very good served on roast beef sandwiches.

Sweet and Snappy Cole Slaw

2 cups shredded cabbage
½ cup chopped green onion
½ cup chopped parsley
¼ cup oil
3 tablespoons vinegar
2½ tablespoons sugar
1 teaspoon salt

Place cabbage, green onion, and parsley in a salad bowl. Combine remaining ingredients and pour over vegetables. (Vegetables and dressing can be prepared separately on Saturday and mixed on Sunday.) Salad keeps well combined ahead and stored covered in the refrigerator. Serves 6.

Cauliflower Slaw

1 large head cauliflower, cut in bite-size pieces
1 cup sliced radishes
½ cup chopped green onions
1 can (about 5 ounces) water chestnuts, sliced thin
1 cup mayonnaise or salad dressing
1 cup sour cream
¼ cup caraway seeds (optional)
1 package dry salad dressing mix (ranch, blue cheese, or garlic flavor)

Toss cauliflower, radishes, onions, and water chestnuts together. Combine remaining ingredients and stir into vegetables. Marinate in refrigerator at least 2 hours or overnight. Serves 10 to 12.

24-Hour Cabbage Salad

1 cup vinegar
1½ cups sugar
1 tablespoon unflavored gelatin softened in ¼ cup cold water
1 teaspoon celery seed
1 teaspoon salt
¼ teaspoon pepper
1 cup salad oil
1 large cabbage, chopped fine

2 green peppers, chopped
2 carrots, grated
1 onion, grated

Heat vinegar and sugar; cook until sugar is dissolved. Remove from heat and add the gelatin softened in the cold water; stir until dissolved. Add celery seed, salt, and pepper. Cool until mixture is consistency of cream. Add salad oil and stir or shake until well mixed. Combine cabbage, peppers, carrots, and onion. Mix dressing into vegetables and refrigerate for 24 hours. Serves 10 to 12.

Pickled Beets and Eggs

½ cup vinegar
½ cup water
1 tablespoon sugar
½ teaspoon salt
Pepper to taste
8 to 12 hard-boiled eggs, peeled
1 jar (16 ounces) pickled beets with juice

Combine vinegar, water, sugar, salt, and pepper. Add eggs and beets and refrigerate at least overnight. Drain (reserve juice) to serve. Serves 8 to 12. May be served as a salad, hors d'oeuvre, or snack, or on a relish plate. Reserved juice may be reused to marinate additional eggs, if desired.

Green Bean Potato Dill Salad

2 pounds small red potatoes
1½ pounds fresh green beans, snapped into bite-size pieces
⅓ cup white vinegar
¼ cup chopped onion
2 teaspoons salt
1 teaspoon dill weed
1 teaspoon sugar
Freshly ground pepper to taste
3 hard-boiled eggs, chopped
1 cup sour cream

Cook unpeeled potatoes in water to cover until just tender; cool, peel, and slice thinly into a large bowl. Cook green beans just until tender. Drain and cool quickly; add to potatoes. In a small mixing bowl, combine vinegar, onion, salt, dill weed, sugar, and pepper. Pour over potatoes and green beans and toss to coat evenly. Gently fold in eggs and sour cream. Cover with plastic wrap and chill. Serves 8 to 10.

Chicken Won Ton Salad

6 chicken breasts, skinned
1 bottle (10 ounces) Kikkoman Teriyaki Sauce
1 medium head iceberg lettuce, torn in pieces
8 to 10 large leaves romaine or red leaf lettuce, torn in pieces
6 to 8 green onions, sliced
¼ cup slivered almonds, toasted
¼ cup sesame seeds
½ package (16 ounces) won ton skins

On the day before serving, place chicken breasts in a baking dish with the Teriyaki sauce and bake at 300° F. for 1 hour, turning every half hour. Cool and dice. Place back in sauce for a few hours. Drain and store in a plastic bag overnight. Cut stack of won ton skins into 4 strips or squares. Separate and fry in hot oil until light brown. Drain on paper towels and set aside. When ready to serve, put lettuce in a large bowl and top with chicken and then remaining ingredients. Toss with dressing (below). A delightful addition is 4 large handfuls of cooked rice sticks (available in Oriental food store). Serves 8 to 10.

Dressing

¾ cup salad oil
1 tablespoon sesame seed oil (no substitute)
½ cup Japanese rice vinegar (no substitute)
⅓ cup sugar
2 teaspoons salt
1 teaspoon coarse pepper
1 teaspoon monosodium glutamate

Combine all ingredients and refrigerate at least several hours or overnight. Makes 1¾ cups dressing.

Taco Salad Extraordinaire

1½ pounds ground beef
Salt and pepper to taste
1 can (30 ounces) dark red kidney beans
   (optional)
1 can (30 ounces) refried beans
1 package taco seasoning mix
1 head iceberg lettuce
1 head romaine lettuce (optional)
3 tomatoes, chopped
1 avocado, sliced thinly
1 can olives, drained
½ cup grated Monterey Jack and Cheddar cheese
Chopped green onions to taste
1 package (12 ounces) tortilla chips
½ cup Italian or onion-garlic salad dressing

Brown hamburger; drain and season to taste with salt and pepper. Drain kidney beans and add to the meat along with the refried beans and taco seasoning. Heat mixture until warm. Toss together lettuce, tomatoes, avocado slices, olives, and cheese. Just before serving, add chips and dressing; toss. Either place several spoonfuls of beef-bean mixture on top of lettuce mixture and serve, or add the beef-bean mixture to the salad and toss again. This is delicious garnished with sour cream, salsa, and guacamole. Serves 10 to 12.

Frozen Cranberry Salad

1 can (16 ounces) whole cranberry sauce
1 can (16 ounces) cranberry jelly
6 tablespoons lemon juice
2 cups whipping cream
½ cup mayonnaise
½ cup powdered sugar
2 cups whole pecans

Stir together cranberry sauce, cranberry jelly, and lemon juice; pour into a ring mold or 13" x 9" glass dish or pan. Freeze. Whip cream and blend in mayonnaise and powdered sugar. Add pecans. Spread over the top of the frozen cranberry sauce and return to the freezer. Unmold on lettuce leaves or cut into squares and serve on lettuce leaves. Serves 12 to 16.

Instant Fruit Salad

1 can (30 ounces) fruit cocktail, drained
1 can (8 ounces) mandarin oranges, drained
1 can (16 ounces) pineapple tidbits or chunks,
   undrained
1 package (3¾ ounces) <u>instant</u> lemon
   pudding powder

Drain fruit cocktail and mandarin oranges. (Reserve juice for other dishes or fruit beverages.) Combine drained fruit cocktail and mandarin oranges with the pineapple tidbits or chunks and the pineapple juice. Sprinkle pudding powder over fruits, and stir until blended. Serve immediately. Serves 12.

Note: Other fruits, such as bananas and seedless grapes, may be added, if desired. Salad may also be made with other flavors of instant pudding, such as coconut, banana, or pineapple.

Lime Wreath Mold

1 can (20 ounces) crushed pineapple, drained
Reserved pineapple syrup
1 package (3 ounces) lime-flavored gelatin
½ cup grated American cheese
½ cup chopped pimiento
½ cup finely chopped celery
⅔ cup chopped walnuts
¼ teaspoon salt
12 to 16 Spanish green olives, stuffed
1 cup heavy cream, whipped

Bring reserved pineapple juice to a boil. Remove from heat, add gelatin, and stir until dissolved. Refrigerate until set but not firm. Stir in rest of ingredients except cream. Whip cream and fold in. Pour into a ring mold and refrigerate to set. (Can be made a day ahead.) Unmold on platter of endive or lettuce. Serves 8 to 10.

Procrastination is my sin,
It brings me naught but sorrow.
I know that I should stop it,
In fact I will—tomorrow!
                              —Gloria Pitzer

Minted Fruit and Vegetable Salad

2 cups cantaloupe balls or cubes
2 cups cucumber cubes
2 cups cherry tomatoes
2 cups seedless grapes (optional)
¼ cup wine vinegar
½ cup oil
1 teaspoon salt
¼ teaspoon pepper
½ teaspoon sugar
1 or 2 tablespoons finely chopped mint leaves
1 or 2 tablespoons finely chopped chives
2 avocados cut in large chunks

Put cantaloupe balls, cucumber cubes, tomatoes, and grapes in a bowl. Make a dressing of vinegar, oil, salt, pepper, sugar, mint leaves, and chives; add to bowl. Cover, and refrigerate overnight. Just before serving, add avocados. Place in salad bowls and garnish each with a mint sprig. Serves 12.

Work for the Lord. The pay isn't much but the retirement plan is out of this world!

Favorite Standby Frozen Salad

1 can (20 ounces) crushed pineapple
1 can (30 ounces) fruit cocktail
1 can (8 ounces) mandarin oranges
1 package (8 ounces) cream cheese
¼ cup salad dressing
1 bunch seedless grapes
1 pint cream, whipped
1 package (10 ounces) miniature white marshmallows
½ cup chopped walnuts or pecans

Drain and combine pineapple, fruit cocktail, and mandarin oranges, reserving juices. Whip fruit juices, cream cheese, and salad dressing in blender. Fold in whipped cream, fruits, marshmallows, and nuts. Pour into an empty milk carton, molds, or paper cupcake containers. Freeze. Unmold by quickly dipping container into hot water. Serves 12.

Artichoke and Rice Salad

2 cups raw rice
4 chicken bouillon cubes
3 cups warm water
2 jars (4 ounces each) marinated artichoke hearts
20 stuffed green olives, sliced
8 green onions, thinly sliced
2 tablespoons green pepper, chopped
1 cup mayonnaise or salad dressing
1 teaspoon curry powder (or to taste)

Place rice in a strainer and rinse thoroughly under running cold water about 2 minutes. In a heavy saucepan, dissolve bouillon cubes in 3 cups warm water. Add rice and bring to a full boil, uncovered, over high heat. Stir; cover with a tight-fitting lid and turn to low. Steam for about 20 minutes or until rice is tender. Put rice in a bowl and let it cool slightly. Drain artichoke hearts, reserving marinade from one jar. Mince artichoke hearts and add to rice with olives, onions, and green pepper. Combine salad dressing, reserved marinade, and curry powder and stir into rice mixture. Chill thoroughly. (Can be made a day ahead.) This is a good dish to serve with ham or barbecued chicken. Serves 8 to 10.

Berry-Cheese Salad

1 package (3 ounces) raspberry-flavored gelatin
1 carton (16 ounces) cottage cheese
1 carton (8 ounces) frozen whipped dessert topping
2 cups fresh raspberries

Stirring constantly, sift gelatin into the cottage cheese. Fold in the dessert topping. Shape half the mixture into a circle on a serving plate. Cover with 1 cup fresh raspberries. Spread with the balance of the cheese mixture and cover with the remaining berries. Chill in the refrigerator until serving time (can be made a day ahead). Serves 6.

Many delicious variations may be made with any well-drained fruit and its corresponding gelatin flavor, such as strawberries, peaches, pineapple, or mandarin oranges.

SALAD DRESSINGS

Thousand Island Dressing

1 cup salad oil
½ cup tarragon vinegar
½ cup cider vinegar
¼ cup catsup
½ cup chili sauce
¼ cup sugar
1 teaspoon salt
1 teaspoon dry mustard
1 clove garlic, mashed
1 small purple onion, finely diced

Combine all ingredients in mixing bowl and mix well. Refrigerate overnight or longer. Yield: 4 cups.

Blue Cheese Dressing

1½ cups buttermilk
2 cups mayonnaise
1 teaspoon parsley flakes
1 teaspoon onion powder
½ teaspoon garlic powder
¼ teaspoon black pepper
1 teaspoon salt
1 tablespoon onion flakes (optional)
1 cup (4 ounces) blue cheese, crumbled

Mix well the buttermilk and mayonnaise (do not mix in blender). Add remaining spices and cheese. Refrigerate. Excellent topping on baked potatoes or as chip dip. Dressing may also be made without blue cheese, if desired. Yield: 4 cups.

Honey Lemon Dressing

2 tablespoons fresh lemon juice
2 tablespoons honey

Combine lemon juice and honey, and mix well. Spoon over fruit salad and toss. Also good on fresh bib lettuce.

Lemon Fruit Dressing

1 egg, well beaten
⅓ cup pineapple juice
½ cup sugar
2 tablespoons cornstarch
2 tablespoons lemon juice
1 cup whipping cream, whipped stiff

In a saucepan, combine egg, pineapple juice, sugar, and cornstarch. Cook over medium heat, stirring constantly, until thick (about 5 to 7 minutes). Add lemon juice and cook 2 minutes more. Let mixture cool; then fold in whipped cream. Yield: 2 cups. Serve on fruit salad or as a dip for a fruit platter.

The best thing you can give to your enemy is forgiveness; to your opponent, tolerance; to a friend, your heart; to your child, good example; to a father, deference; to a mother, conduct that will make her proud of you; to yourself, respect; to all men, charity. (Francis Maitland Balfour)

Raspberry Creme Dressing

1 small package (3 ounces) cream cheese
1 tablespoon lemon juice
1 tablespoon grated lemon peel
¼ teaspoon salt
½ cup raspberry jam
½ cup whipping cream, whipped stiff

Blend together all ingredients except cream; then fold in whipped cream. This makes a delicious dip for a fruit platter or dressing for fruit salad. Yield: 2 cups.

VEGETABLES

Rotkohl (German Red Cabbage)

¼ pound bacon, finely diced
   (or 4 tablespoons bacon fat)
1 medium onion, chopped
1 small head red cabbage (about 8 cups
   finely chopped or coarsely grated)
2 large baking apples, grated
   (or ½ cup applesauce)
1 teaspoon salt
½ teaspoon ground cloves
½ cup brown sugar (or to taste)
⅓ cup vinegar (or to taste)
1 cup water

In a large, heavy kettle, cook bacon with onion until most of fat is rendered. Add remaining ingredients and stir until all is hot. Turn to low and continue to cook at least 2 hours, stirring occasionally, and adding water, if necessary, to keep from burning. When ready to serve, boil most of juice out. Serves 8. This is a good vegetable to cook a day ahead. Refrigerate in a covered container. Reheat and serve.

Scalloped Cabbage

1 medium head cabbage, sliced thin
   and chopped
3 tablespoons butter
Salt and pepper to taste
1 egg, beaten until foamy
½ cup cream or half-and-half
1½ cups crushed soda cracker crumbs
2 to 4 tablespoons melted butter

Place cabbage in a saucepan with a very small amount of water. Cover and steam 5 minutes. Pour off water. Stir butter, salt, and pepper into cabbage. Blend egg and cream and pour over cabbage. Place in a casserole. Combine crumbs and butter and sprinkle over cabbage. Bake at 325° F. for 35 minutes or until liquid is set. This is good made with shredded carrots instead of cabbage, with a little sage added. Serves 6 to 8.

Creamed Cauliflower and Peas

2 tablespoons butter, melted
2 tablespoons flour
1 cup milk
¼ teaspoon salt
Dash of pepper
1 package (10 ounces) frozen tender green peas
1 head cauliflower, separated into flowerets
1 cup shredded Cheddar cheese

Blend the butter and flour together in a saucepan until smooth. Add milk and cook over medium heat until thick, stirring constantly. Add salt and pepper. Cook the peas according to package directions; drain and add to the white sauce. Meanwhile, cook cauliflower until tender in a small amount of salted water; drain. Place the cauliflower in the bottom of a serving dish. Pour the creamed peas over the top. Sprinkle with the cheese and serve immediately. Also good with sliced mushrooms. Serves 6 to 8.

Ratatouille

½ cup oil
1 medium onion, sliced
2 green peppers, cut in chunks
2 small or 1 large eggplant, peeled and sliced
   ½-inch thick
4 to 6 tomatoes, peeled and cut up
2 zucchini, sliced
1 tablespoon parsley, chopped
1 large clove garlic, minced or crushed
Pinch each of marjoram and basil
Salt and pepper to taste

Heat oil in a large saucepan or 12-inch skillet. Add the vegetables; cover and simmer gently for 30 minutes, stirring occasionally. Uncover, add rest of ingredients, and continue to simmer 10 to 15 minutes or until contents are well mixed. Serve hot or cold as a first course or with bread and cheese for Sunday supper. Serves 8 to 10.

Carrots Sweet and Sour

2 pounds carrots, peeled and cut diagonally
   in ½-inch slices
1 green pepper, cut in chunks
1 large onion, chopped
1 can (10 ounces) condensed tomato soup
½ cup salad oil
½ cup vinegar
1 teaspoon salt
¾ cup sugar

Steam the carrots just until tender-crisp in a small amount of water. Combine the rest of the ingredients in a saucepan and bring to a boil for one minute. Pour hot over the drained carrots. Store in the refrigerator overnight. Keeps well a week or so. May be served either hot or cold as a vegetable or relish. Serves 8.

Vegetable Medley

4 medium onions, cut in thin wedges
1 pound carrots, sliced about ¼-inch thick
1 medium cauliflower (about 2 pounds),
   cut into flowerets
1 package (10 ounces) frozen whole green beans,
   partially defrosted
1 package (10 ounces) frozen artichoke hearts,
   partially defrosted, or 1 bottle (6 ounces)
   marinated artichoke hearts
½ cup salad oil
½ cup cider or tarragon vinegar
1 tablespoon sugar
1 tablespoon salt
½ teaspoon crushed red pepper

In a large saucepan or Dutch oven put about 2 cups of water. Layer the vegetables in the order listed, starting with the onions and finishing with the artichoke hearts. (If using marinated hearts, don't cook; just add when you add dressing.) Bring to a boil; cover, reduce heat to low, and steam 10 minutes or until tender-crisp. Drain. Mix the vinegar, oil, sugar, salt, and red pepper. Put vegetables in a large bowl. Pour marinade over vegetables, and cover bowl. Vegetables may be eaten at once while warm, or refrigerated. They may be reheated and served hot or chilled on a bed of lettuce or red cabbage leaves. Serves 12 to 15.

Garden Medley

2 tablespoons butter
2 small yellow crookneck squash, thinly diced
   (don't peel)
2 small onions, thinly sliced
1 medium ear of corn, blanched and
   cut from cob
½ to ¾ cup small spinach leaves
1 green pepper, slivered
1 medium tomato, peeled and coarsely chopped
1 strip hot pepper, slivered (optional)
Salt
Pepper
Mace
Curry powder

Melt butter in a large skillet. Add vegetables and stir-fry until tender-crisp. Season with salt, fresh ground pepper, and a dash of mace and curry powder. Serve immediately. Serves 6.

Green Spinach Croustade

½ pound phyllo dough*
1 package (10 ounces) frozen chopped spinach
½ pound feta cheese, crumbled
½ pound large-curd cream-style cottage cheese
1 package (3 ounces) cream cheese
¾ cup green onions, chopped
3 eggs, slightly beaten
¼ cup olive oil
¼ cup salad oil
½ cup butter

Thaw phyllo dough overnight in refrigerator. Thaw and drain spinach. In a medium-size bowl, mix spinach, feta, cottage cheese, cream cheese, and green onions. Add eggs and oils. Set aside. Melt butter. Brush melted butter on a 9-inch square cake pan. Spread a layer of phyllo dough in bottom of cake pan. Brush phyllo with melted butter; then add another layer of phyllo, and continue layering phyllo with butter until there are 4 layers of each. Spread with a layer of spinach filling. Add 2 more layers of phyllo and melted butter, then filling, repeating with phyllo and spinach until filling is gone. (This should make about 5 or 6 layers of filling between the phyllo layers.) Top with four layers of phyllo and butter. (Dish may be refrigerated or frozen at this point.)

Bake at 350° F. for 45 minutes. (If dish has been refrigerated or frozen, add 10 to 20 minutes baking time.) Cool slightly and cut into diamond-shaped pieces, with the size of the piece depending on whether it is to be served as an appetizer or as a vegetable accompaniment to the meal. Serve either warm or cold. Serves 8.

*Phyllo is available in the frozen-food section of specialty grocery stores and supermarkets. It is spelled variously as filo, fillo, and phyllo.

Spinach Pudding

- 2 packages (10 ounces each) frozen chopped spinach
- 2 cups cream-style cottage cheese
- 2 eggs
- ⅓ cup Parmesan cheese
- 1 teaspoon salt

Cook spinach according to package directions. Drain. Mix all ingredients together. Put in a 2-quart baking dish or ring mold. Bake at 350° for 30 minutes or until set. Serves 8 to 10.

Broccoli-Cheese Casserole

- 1 jar (8 ounces) Cheez Whiz
- 1 can (10 ounces) condensed cream of mushroom soup
- 1 cup chopped celery
- 1 package (10 ounces) frozen chopped broccoli, thawed
- ½ cup chopped onion
- ¼ teaspoon salt
- 6 tablespoons margarine, melted
- 1½ cups <u>instant</u> rice, added dry from package

In a medium-size mixing bowl, mix together the Cheez Whiz and cream of mushroom soup. Combine the rest of the ingredients in a 9-inch square casserole dish, and stir in the cheese-soup mixture. (Can be refrigerated at this point.) Bake at 325° F. for 35 minutes (allow an extra 10 to 15 minutes if dish has been refrigerated). Serves 8.

Broccoli-Cheese Scallop

- 4 packages (10 ounces each) frozen broccoli spears
- 2 cups shredded Swiss cheese
- ⅔ cup mayonnaise
- 1 tablespoon minced onion
- ½ teaspoon salt
- ¼ teaspoon pepper
- 1 teaspoon prepared mustard

Cook broccoli in a small amount of water until it is tender-crisp. Drain. Spread broccoli in bottom of a 9" x 13" baking dish or pan. Combine the remaining ingredients and spread over broccoli. (Can be refrigerated at this point.) Bake at 350° F. for 15 to 20 minutes (allow an extra 10 to 15 minutes if dish has been refrigerated). Serves 12.

Carrot and Cabbage Casserole

- 1 medium head cabbage, cut in chunks
- 4 to 6 medium carrots, cut diagonally in ½-inch slices
- ¼ cup butter
- ¼ cup flour
- 2 cups milk
- Salt and pepper
- 2 cups shredded Cheddar cheese

In separate pans, steam the cabbage and the carrots in a small amount of water until tender. Make a white sauce by stirring the flour and butter together in a heavy saucepan over low heat. Add the milk and cook, stirring constantly, until thick. Season to taste with salt and pepper. In a buttered 2-quart casserole dish, arrange in alternate layers the cabbage, carrots, white sauce, and shredded cheese. (Can be refrigerated at this point.) Bake at 325° F. for 15 to 20 minutes or until bubbly.

Variation

Top with buttered bread crumbs, or spread a can of French-fried onion rings over the top for the last 5 minutes of baking.

Cauliflower with Almonds

1 large head cauliflower
¼ cup butter
½ cup slivered almonds
1 cup soft bread crumbs
1 clove garlic, minced

Steam cauliflower until tender, about 30 minutes. Meanwhile, sauté almonds, bread crumbs, and garlic in the butter until the almonds are golden and the crumbs are crisp. Stir frequently. Drain cauliflower and put it in a serving dish. Sprinkle crumb mixture over the cauliflower. Serves 6.

Summer Special

½ cup butter
¼ cup diced green pepper
¼ cup chopped onion
4 small zucchini, cut in 1-inch cubes
2 ears corn, cut from cobs
6 medium tomatoes, peeled and cut into eighths
1 teaspoon basil
½ teaspoon dill seed
1 teaspoon salt

Melt butter in a heavy skillet. Add pepper and onion, and sauté until onion is transparent. Add zucchini, corn, tomatoes, and seasonings. Cook 10 minutes, stirring occasionally. Serves 8 to 10. *Note:* All vegetables except tomatoes may be prepared on Saturday.

Baked Beans

¼ to ½ pound bacon, cut into small pieces
1 onion, chopped
1 green pepper, chopped
1 can (30 ounces) pork and beans
1 tablespoon Worcestershire sauce
1 tablespoon mustard
½ cup brown sugar
½ cup catsup
1 can (20 ounces) crushed pineapple, drained

Brown together the bacon, onion, and green pepper. Mix with the rest of ingredients in a large casserole dish or bean pot. Bake about 3 hours at 250° to 300° F. Serves 8 to 10.

Note: This casserole can be prepared on Saturday and then baked with ham while you attend church on Sunday. Serve with Boston brown bread and your favorite salad.

Sour Cream Potato Casserole

6 potatoes
⅓ cup chopped onion
1 can (10 ounces) condensed cream of chicken soup
1 cup sour cream
4 tablespoons butter or margarine, melted
½ cup grated cheese
½ cup Ritz Cracker crumbs

Boil potatoes in salted water until tender. Drain. Dice when cool enough to handle. In a 2-quart casserole, place potatoes and onions. Combine soup, sour cream, and butter, and stir until smooth. Pour over potatoes and onions. Combine cheese and crumbs and sprinkle on top. (Can be refrigerated at this point.) Bake at 350° F. until bubbly, approximately 30 minutes. Serves 6.

Fast Cheesy Potatoes

6 boiled potatoes
1 can (10 ounces) condensed Cheddar cheese soup
1 tablespoon butter
Salt and pepper to taste

Slice the boiled potatoes and arrange in a 2-quart casserole dish. Pour the soup over the top. Dot with butter; add salt and pepper to taste. (Can be refrigerated at this point.) Bake at 350° F. for 30 minutes or until hot. Serves 6 to 8.

Quick method: Slice raw potatoes ¼-inch thick into a skillet; add a little water and salt. Boil for 5 minutes; drain. Pour soup over top, dot with butter, and heat on stove burner. Serve in the skillet.

Cream-Cheesy Potatoes

Dry potato flakes, reconstituted according to
 package directions for 12 servings
1 package (8 ounces) cream cheese
2 eggs
1 tablespoon dry minced onion
1 tablespoon parsley flakes
2 tablespoons butter or margarine, melted
Paprika

Prepare potatoes. Beat in cheese and onions. Add eggs and blend well. Stir in parsley. Spoon into a 9" x 13" x 2" baking dish and smooth top with back of tablespoon. Pour melted butter over and sprinkle with paprika. (May be refrigerated at this point.) Bake at 350° F. for 25 to 30 minutes. Serves 12.

Pan-fried Potatoes

Scrub but do not peel 6 medium potatoes. Slice ¼-inch thick across the narrow way. Melt 4 tablespoons butter in a 12-inch skillet over medium heat. Add potato slices and cook 20 minutes, turning occasionally, until potatoes are tender and golden brown. Sprinkle with 1 teaspoon salt and pepper to taste.

Potato Pancakes

6 large potatoes, peeled and quartered
1 large onion, grated
2 eggs
½ cup sour cream
2 tablespoons flour
¼ cup fine bread crumbs
Salt and pepper to taste

Place potatoes in a bowl of water to cover. Grate potatoes a few at a time with fine blade or on medium side of vegetable grater. Return to bowl of water to cover. Combine remaining ingredients; drain potatoes and mix with other ingredients. Check consistency of mixture; it should be neither too watery nor too thick. If thin, add more flour; if thick, add more sour cream. Drop by heaping spoonfuls into hot oil about ½-inch deep and fry to golden brown. Drain. Keep warm in oven set at 350° F. until all pancakes are cooked. These are very good served with grated cheese, crumbled sausage, or catsup, or as a side dish with meat or an omelette. Serves 6 to 8.

Yum-Yum Potatoes

3 cups cream-style cottage cheese
¾ cup sour cream
4 cups mashed potatoes (do not use instant
 mashed potatoes and do not add milk
 or butter)
1½ tablespoons finely grated onion
¼ teaspoon pepper
Salt to taste
¼ cup Parmesan cheese

Whip in blender until smooth cottage cheese and sour cream; add to the mashed potatoes. Stir in onion, pepper, and salt. Spoon into a buttered 2-quart casserole. Brush top with melted butter and sprinkle with Parmesan cheese. (Can be refrigerated at this point.) Bake at 350° F. for 30 minutes. Serves 6 to 8.

Variation

Top with French-fried onions or chow mein noodles. When using onions or noodles, watch carefully; they burn easily and quickly.

Easy Pilaf

¼ cup butter, melted
1 medium green pepper, chopped
1 cup tomatoes, cut in small pieces
1 clove garlic, minced
1 teaspoon salt
1 cup sliced mushrooms (fresh or canned)
Pepper to taste
2 cups beef stock or boullion
½ cup raw rice (not instant)

Combine all ingredients in a 9" x 12" casserole dish. (Can be refrigerated at this point.) Bake 1 hour at 350° F. Serves 8 to 12.

Noodles and Nuts

1 cup butter
1½ cups slivered almonds
½ cup poppy seeds
¾ teaspoon salt
2 packages (8 ounces each) krinkle noodles

In a skillet over medium heat, melt butter. Add almonds and sauté until nuts are golden brown. Stir in poppy seeds and salt. Cook noodles according to package directions; drain. Pour nut mixture over noodles. Serves 12.

Salsa Verde Pasta

2 cups coarsely chopped fresh spinach,
    or 1 package (10 ounces) frozen spinach,
    thawed
1 cup chopped Italian parsley (also called
    Chinese parsley)
½ cup oil*
¾ cup grated Parmesan cheese
½ cup grated Romano cheese
⅓ cup pine nuts (optional)
3 tablespoons dry basil
2 small cloves garlic, minced
1 teaspoon salt
Dash of pepper
1 package (8 ounces) noodles, cooked according
    to package directions

Put all ingredients but noodles into blender container. Cover and blend until smooth. Heat and serve over hot, buttered noodles. Sauce can be made ahead and stored in refrigerator.

*Olive oil is preferred, but it must be very high quality, such as Star brand.

Spanish Tortilla

1 cup milk
6 eggs
Salt and pepper to taste
3 tablespoons oil
4 to 5 potatoes, boiled, peeled, and chopped
1 medium onion, chopped

In a bowl, combine milk, eggs, and salt and pepper. Pour egg mixture into hot oiled skillet. Add potatoes and onion. Cover; cook over medium heat. When mixture is browned on bottom and fairly solid, invert on a flat plate to turn, and slide back into skillet; cook on second side. Cut in wedges. Serves 6 to 8.

Variations

Add as desired one or more of the following ingredients: shredded Monterey Jack cheese, ham, chicken, green peppers, mushrooms, minced parsley.

For a very light, fluffy omelet, separate the eggs. Combine egg yolks with milk, salt, and pepper. Beat the egg whites until fluffy and fold into milk-and-yolk mixture. Then fold in potatoes and onions and proceed as above. Serves 8.

Basic Rice Luncheon Dish

2 cups cooked rice, cooled
1 cup milk
2 tablespoons butter
½ clove garlic, minced
2 tablespoons onion, chopped
¼ cup parsley
¼ cup Cheddar cheese, diced
4 eggs, separated

Mix together all ingredients but egg whites. Beat egg whites well and fold into mixture. Place in greased 9-inch square pan and bake at 350° F. for 45 minutes. Cut into squares and serve topped with sauce (below). Serves 8.

Sauce

½ cup butter
½ cup flour
3 cups milk
½ teaspoon salt
1 jar (4 ounces) pimiento cheese
1 small bottle stuffed green olives, sliced
2 cans (6 ounces each) mushrooms, drained

Make white sauce by melting butter and flour together; add milk. Cook over medium heat, stirring constantly until thick. Add the rest of the ingredients and heat.

CHICKEN MARBELLA

This was the first main-course dish to be offered at The Silver Palate, and the distinctive colors and flavors of the prunes, olives and capers have kept it a favorite for years. It's good hot or at room temperature. When prepared with small drumsticks and wings, it makes a delicious hors d'oeuvre.

The overnight marination is essential to the moistness of the finished product: the chicken keeps and even improves over several days of refrigeration; it travels well and makes excellent picnic fare.

Since Chicken Marbella is such a spectacular party dish, we give quantities to serve 10 to 12, but the recipe can successfully be divided to make a smaller amount if you wish.

4 chickens, 2½ pounds each, quartered
1 head of garlic, peeled and finely puréed
¼ cup dried oregano
coarse salt and freshly ground black pepper to taste
½ cup red wine vinegar
½ cup olive oil
1 cup pitted prunes
½ cup pitted Spanish green olives
½ cup capers with a bit of juice
6 bay leaves
1 cup brown sugar
1 cup white wine
¼ cup Italian parsley or fresh coriander (cilantro), finely
  chopped

1. In a large bowl combine chicken quarters, garlic, oregano, pepper and coarse salt to taste, vinegar, olive oil, prunes, olives, capers and juice, and bay leaves. Cover and let marinate, refrigerated, overnight.

2. Preheat oven to 350°F.

3. Arrange chicken in a single layer in one or two large, shallow baking pans and spoon marinade over it evenly. Sprinkle chicken pieces with brown sugar and pour white wine around them.

4. Bake for 50 minutes to 1 hour, basting frequently with pan juices. Chicken is done when thigh pieces, pricked with a fork at their thickest, yield clear yellow (rather than pink) juice.

5. With a slotted spoon transfer chicken, prunes, olives and capers to a serving platter. Moisten with a few spoonfuls of pan juices and sprinkle generously with parsley or cilantro. Pass remaining pan juices in a sauceboat.

6. To serve Chicken Marbella cold, cool to room tempera-

THE CHICKEN CHART

BROILERS:
1 to 2½ pounds; young chickens with little fat.

BROILERS/FRYERS:
2½ to 3½ pounds. Butchers use these terms interchangeably. If you prepare them well, these chickens may be cooked either way. Look for yellow fat and plump breasts.

ROASTERS/PULLETS:
3½ to 6½ pounds; good for roasting, baking, barbecuing and quick cooking. Bred for tenderness and very meaty.

HENS AND FOWL:
Up to 8 pounds; best for stock or chicken salad. They require longer and slower cooking but are by far the most flavorful.

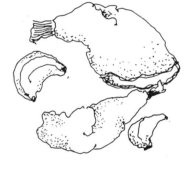

COUNTRY WEEKEND LUNCH

Cheese Straws
Crudités and assorted dips

Chicken Marbella
Semolina Bread
Boucheron cheese

Lime Mousse
Chocolate Chip Cookies

Golden Mushroom Puff

10 slices white bread
6 eggs
3 cups milk
¾ teaspoon dry mustard
½ teaspoon salt
2½ cups (8 ounces) shredded sharp cheese
2 cups sliced fresh mushrooms

Remove crusts from bread; cut slices into cubes. Beat eggs, milk, mustard, and salt. Stir in bread cubes, cheese, and mushrooms. Pour into an 11½" x 7½" baking dish. (Can be refrigerated at this point.) Bake, uncovered, at 325° F. for 45 minutes or until center is set. Serves 8.

Cheese Puff

6 eggs
½ cup flour
1 teaspoon baking powder
½ teaspoon salt
1 cup milk
8 ounces cream-style cottage cheese
1 package (3 ounces) cream cheese, cubed small
6 tablespoons butter or margarine
1 pound Monterey Jack cheese, cubed small

In a large bowl, beat eggs until fluffy; add flour, baking powder, salt, and milk, and beat until

_____

Success comes in cans, failure in can'ts.

_____

smooth. Stir in the rest of the ingredients. Pour into a buttered 9-inch square baking pan. (Can be refrigerated at this point.) Bake at 350° F. about 45 minutes or until a knife inserted near the center comes out clean. (If dish has been refrigerated, allow 10 minutes additional baking time.) Serves 6 to 8.

_____

To bring a child up in the way he should go, travel that way yourself once in a while. (Josh Billings)

_____

Chili Relleno Casserole

¾ pound Monterey Jack cheese, grated
¾ pound Cheddar cheese, grated
2 cans (7 ounces each) mild green chilies
2 tablespoons flour
4 eggs
1 can (13 ounces) evaporated milk
1 can (8 ounces) tomato sauce
1 can (7 ounces) green chili salsa

Combine the cheeses. In a 9" x 13" casserole dish, layer 1 can of chilies (opened and seeded) with half of the cheeses. Add the other can of chilies and the other half of the cheeses. In blender combine flour, eggs, and canned milk. Pour over layers of chilies and cheese. Bake at 350° F. for 25 minutes. Mix tomato sauce and green chili salsa and pour over top of casserole. Return to oven and bake at 350° F. for additional 30 minutes or until firm. Serves 10.

Ye are the salt of the earth

Dips, Sauces, and Condiments

DIPS, SAUCES, AND CONDIMENTS

Traveling Taco Dip

1 can (30 ounces) refried beans
½ package dry taco seasoning mix
1 can (4 ounces) chopped green chilies
1 cup guacamole (below)
1 can (4 ounces) sliced ripe olives
1 cup sour cream
¼ cup sliced green onions
1 cup grated Colby or favorite Cheddar cheese
1 cup chopped tomatoes
Alfalfa sprouts

Stir beans and taco mix together and spread in a 10-inch pie plate or on a platter. Layer the rest of the ingredients over beans in the order given, ending with a sprinkling of sprouts. Serve cold with a basket of large corn or tortilla chips to dip with.

Guacamole

Mash 1 ripe avocado. Stir in 2 tablespoons chopped onion, ¼ cup chopped tomato, 2 table-spoons sour cream, and salt to taste.

Sweet Mustard Sauce

½ cup butter, melted
1 cup prepared mustard
1 cup sugar
1 can (10 ounces) condensed tomato soup
½ cup vinegar
½ cup water
4 eggs, slightly beaten

Combine all ingredients except eggs and stir until smooth. Stir in eggs and cook over medium heat until thick, stirring constantly. This is delicious with ham or roast beef and as a spread on sandwiches. Makes about 1 quart.

Chili Con Queso Dip

3 large onions, chopped
3 cloves garlic, minced
3 cans (4 ounces each) diced green chilies, drained
3 cans (16 ounces each) tomatoes, drained
2 pounds Velveta cheese, cubed
Salt to taste

Combine onions, garlic, chilies, and tomatoes in a saucepan and simmer, covered, 1 hour. Add cheese and salt and stir until melted and well blended. (Mixture may be processed in a blender to make a smooth sauce.) Serve hot with corn chips. Dip is also good as a topping on Mexican food. Yield: 2 quarts.

It's true that you can't take it with you, but folks ought to remember that how you got it may determine where you go.

Excellent Barbecue Sauce

2 tablespoons Worcestershire sauce
1 bottle (16 ounces) A-1 Sauce
1 bottle (8 ounces) Heinz 57 Sauce
¾ cup vinegar
3 tablespoons Tabasco sauce
1 dry Spanish pepper, crushed
2 tablespoons minced garlic
1 tablespoon crushed dry parsley
1 cup butter

Combine all ingredients in a saucepan and bring to a boil; boil 1 minute. Store in refrigerator and use on ribs, shishkabobs, ham, chicken, or hamburgers.

Grampa's Homemade Mustard

¼ cup sugar
2½ cups water
1 teaspoon salt
½ teaspoon black pepper
4 teaspoons dry mustard
¼ cup flour
1 teaspoon tumeric
½ cup cider vinegar
2 cups (1 pint) sour cream
2 eggs, beaten

In a saucepan, combine all ingredients except eggs and sour cream; blend well. Bring to a boil and cook, stirring constantly, until thick. Pour a little of the hot liquid into the eggs; stir until blended, and return to hot mixture. Cook, stirring, for 2 minutes. Cool. Add sour cream. Store in glass jar in refrigerator. Makes about 6 cups.

Yugoslavian Caviar

1 large eggplant
6 tablespoons parsley, dried or fresh
6 cloves garlic
2 tablespoons pepper
2 tablespoons salt
¼ cup olive oil
¼ cup vinegar

Bake eggplant at 350° F. for 1 hour. Peel when cooled. Chop eggplant, parsley, and garlic very fine and add salt, pepper, oil, and vinegar. Cover and store in refrigerator. Serve on beef sandwiches or with meat entrées. Keeps 3 to 4 weeks.

One good idea put to use is worth a hundred buzzing around in the back of your head.

Cheese Shrimp Dip

2 packages (8 ounces each) cream cheese
1 cup sour cream
Juice of ½ lemon
1 teaspoon dehydrated onion (or to taste)
2 cans (4 ounces each) small shrimp
1 can (8 ounces) water chestnuts, diced
2 tablespoons mayonnaise

Mix all of the ingredients together. Serve as a dip or spread with crackers or vegetables.

Dill Dip

1 pint sour cream
1 cup mayonnaise
2 tablespoons minced dry onions
2 tablespoons dried parsley flakes
2 tablespoons dill weed, crushed
1 tablespoon Spice Island Beau Monde blend*

Blend all together and let stand in refrigerator at least 2 hours, or preferably overnight. Serve with raw vegetables or chips.

*Spice Island Beau Monde is a blend of celery, salt, sugar, and onion.

Many people are unhappy because they are poor mathematicians. They have never learned to count their blessings.

Tartar Sauce

⅔ cup mayonnaise
1 teaspoon grated onion
1 teaspoon dried parsley
2 tablespoons chopped chives
1 tablespoon chopped sweet or dill pickles
2 dashes Tabasco sauce

Combine all ingredients. Allow to season in refrigerator. Makes 1 cup.

Let us break bread together

Breads and Sandwiches

BREADS

Never-Fail Bread

2 tablespoons shortening
2½ teaspoons salt
4 tablespoons sugar
1 cup hot evaporated milk
1¼ cups hot water
1 package (1 tablespoon) dry yeast
6 cups white flour

In a large bowl, mix the shortening, salt, and 2 tablespoons of the sugar. Add the hot milk and 1 cup of the hot water. Let cool to lukewarm. In a small bowl put ¼ cup warm water, 2 tablespoons sugar, and yeast. Let stand for 5 minutes. Add the dissolved yeast and 3 cups flour to the first mixture and beat well. Mix in 2 more cups of flour. Turn out onto a lightly floured board, and knead for 4 to 5 minutes. Let rest 10 minutes. Add just enough of the remaining flour so that the dough is not sticky. Resume kneading until the dough is smooth and elastic (shiny with gluten). Put dough in a large greased bowl. Cover and let rise in a warm place until double in bulk. Punch down and shape into 2 loaves. Place in greased loaf pans. Cover and let double in bulk again. Preheat oven to 425° F. Bake bread 15 minutes, then reduce heat to 375° F. and bake 20 to 30 minutes longer. Remove from pans and cool on racks.

Variation

To make Cheese Bread, mix 1½ cups grated Cheddar cheese or other sharp cheese with the last flour added.

The bread that you store up belongs to the hungry; the cloak that lies in your chest belongs to the naked; and the gold that you have hidden in the ground belongs to the poor. (St. Basil)

No-knead, No-work, No-fail Whole Wheat Bread

7½ cups whole wheat flour
2 packages (2 tablespoons) dry yeast
1 cup warm water
1 tablespoon honey
2 teaspoons salt
4 tablespoons molasses
3 cups warm water

Place the flour in a warm (not hot) oven while you dissolve the yeast. In a mixing bowl put 1 cup warm water (110° F.); add honey and yeast. Let stand 5 minutes. Add the flour (be sure it is just warm, not hot), salt, molasses, and warm water, and mix well. Grease two loaf pans, and spoon batter into them. Let rise in a warm place, about 15 minutes. Preheat oven to 375° F. Bake bread for 30 to 40 minutes. Remove from pans and cool on racks.

Onion Herb Batter Bread

½ cup milk
1½ tablespoons sugar
1 teaspoon salt
2¼ tablespoons margarine
1 package (1 tablespoon) dry yeast
½ cup warm water
2½ cups flour
1 cup finely chopped onions
2 teaspoons dill weed

Scald the milk. Add sugar, salt, and margarine, and cool to lukewarm. Dissolve the yeast in the warm water until bubbly (about 5 minutes). Combine the milk and yeast mixtures. Add the flour, onions, and dill weed. Beat 2 minutes. Place in a greased loaf pan and cover with waxed paper. Let rise until double in bulk. Bake at 350° F. for 1 hour. Remove from pan and cool on a rack.

Quick and Easy Brown Bread

1 package (1 tablespoon) dry yeast
2 cups warm water
2 tablespoons sugar
1 teaspoon salt
4 cups whole wheat flour
White flour

Dissolve yeast in the warm water; add sugar. Let sit until yeast bubbles—about 15 minutes. Add salt and whole wheat flour. Stir in sufficient white flour to make dough stiff enough to knead. Knead dough until it is smooth and slightly shiny. Let rise until double in bulk; punch down and form into 2 small loaves or 1 large loaf. Put loaves into greased loaf pans. Let rise in a warm place until double in bulk. Bake for 25 minutes in oven preheated to 425° F. Remove loaves from pans and cool on racks.

Never-Fail Butter Rolls

4 cups water (part or all can be potato water)
2 packages (2 tablespoons) dry yeast
1 cup sugar
1 cup instant dry milk
6 eggs
1 cup melted butter or margarine, cooled
2 teaspoons salt
8 to 10 cups flour

In a large mixing bowl stir together water, yeast, sugar, and dry milk. Let stand until bubbly. In a separate bowl beat eggs till fluffy; add cooled margarine, and blend well. Add eggs to yeast mixture with 6 cups of the flour and salt; blend. Mix in additional flour until the dough is smooth but still quite soft. (The less flour you use, the more tender the rolls will be.) Let rise until double in bulk. Roll out and form in desired shape. Place rolls on a greased baking pan or cookie sheet and cover with waxed paper. Let rise till double in bulk. Bake at 400° F. until golden brown. Makes about 6 dozen rolls.

Note: If you have mashed potatoes or potato flakes on hand, add them for a heartier, moister roll. This recipe also makes delicious cinnamon rolls and scones.

Variations

Raisin Filling for Danish Rolls: Mix together 1 cup raisins, 1½ cups water, 1 tablespoon vinegar, ¼ teaspoon salt, and ½ cup sugar. Mix together ¼ cup water and 2 tablespoons cornstarch, and add to raisin mixture. Cook over medium heat until thick, stirring constantly. Remove from heat and add 1 tablespoon butter, ½ cup chopped pecans, 1 teaspoon vanilla, 1 teaspoon lemon flavoring, 1½ teaspoons cinnamon, and ¼ teaspoon nutmeg. Cool. Roll out dough (above) into a 9″ x 12″ rectangle about ½-inch thick. Spread filling almost to edges. Roll up like a jelly roll and place on a large cookie sheet in a crescent shape. Cut two-thirds of the way through the roll every 1½ inches and flare out in a half twist. Let rise until double in bulk. Bake as directed above. Drizzle over the top a frosting made of confectioners' sugar moistened with water and flavored with vanilla.

Onion-Cheese Rolls: Form rolls as desired and brush top with beaten egg. Sprinkle with chopped onions and shredded cheese. For hamburger rolls, brush with beaten egg and sprinkle with sesame or poppy seeds. Bake as directed above.

Orange Crescent Rolls: Blend ¾ cup sugar and ¾ cup butter or margarine, and add 2 tablespoons grated orange rind (or to taste). Roll dough (above) into circles each 9 inches in diameter, and spread a thin layer of orange paste over dough. Cut each circle into 6 to 8 pie-shaped pieces and roll from wide end to point. Place on a greased cookie sheet and form into a crescent shape. Cover and let rise until double in bulk. Bake as directed above.

_____

The Sabbath is the choicest fruit and flower of the week, the Queen whose coming changes the humblest home into a palace. (Judah Halevi)

_____

Granary Bread Sticks

1½ cups triticale flakes or rolled wheat
½ cup milk or water
1 package (1 tablespoon) dry yeast
½ cup warm water
½ cup honey or sugar
1 teaspoon salt
2 cups milk or water
⅓ cup gluten flour
4 cups whole wheat flour
1 cup white flour (or more if needed to make a manageable dough)

In a small mixing bowl, pour ½ cup water or milk over triticale. Set aside. In a large mixing bowl, dissolve yeast in ½ cup warm water. Let stand 5 minutes. Add honey or sugar, salt, 2 cups milk or water, and the flours. Knead about 12 minutes in a bread mixer or by hand until elastic. Knead in the moistened triticale. Put in an oiled bowl, cover, and let rise in a warm place, punching down every 10 minutes for about 1 hour. Form into bread sticks on a greased cookie sheet. Let rise until double in bulk. Preheat oven to 375° F., and bake about 20 to 30 minutes, depending on the size of the sticks.

Cheesy Bread Sticks

2 packages (2 tablespoons) dry yeast
1 cup lukewarm water
2 tablespoons sugar
1 tablespoon salt
2 cups lukewarm water
¼ cup oil
8 cups flour, unsifted
1 cup butter, melted
Parmesan cheese

In a large mixing bowl, dissolve yeast in 1 cup of water with sugar. Let stand 5 minutes. Add the rest of the ingredients except the butter and the cheese. Stir into a dough and knead until smooth and elastic. Cover and let rise. Punch down every 10 minutes for 5 times. Flatten dough on a board and cut into strips. Cover a cookie sheet with foil. Dip the dough strips in melted butter and then roll in Parmesan cheese.

Twist and lay out on foil-covered cookie sheet. Allow to rise about 30 minutes or until double in bulk. Bake at 350° F. for 10 to 15 minutes until golden brown. Bread sticks may be half baked, put in plastic bags, and refrigerated or frozen until needed. Then finish the baking and serve. Makes about 2 dozen long sticks or 4 dozen short ones.

Variation

For French Bread, form dough into 2 loaves, brush with lightly beaten egg whites, and roll in sesame seeds. Place on a cookie sheet and allow to rise until double in bulk. Bake at 400° F. for 35 to 40 minutes.

It's better to wear out. . . than to rust out!

Irish Soda Bread

4 cups sifted whole wheat flour
1½ teaspoons salt
4 teaspoons baking powder
1 teaspoon baking soda
¼ cup brown sugar or honey
½ cup rolled oats (rolled wheat or triticale may also be used)
½ cup butter or margarine
1 cup chopped dates or raisins (optional)
2 cups buttermilk (or use 1¾ cups whole milk and ¼ cup vinegar)

Sift the flour, salt, baking powder, and soda together in a mixing bowl. Stir in brown sugar and rolled oats. Cut in margarine until it looks like coarse meal. Mix in dates or raisins, if desired. At this point bread can be covered and stored in the refrigerator until 40 minutes before serving.

Grease a 10-inch ovenproof skillet (cast iron works well) or use a cookie sheet. Preheat oven to 400° F. Stir buttermilk into flour mixture to make a stiff dough. Knead at least 10 times. Form into a ball, and place into skillet, or, if using a cookie sheet, flatten into about a 10-inch circle. Score almost through the dough with a floured knife to mark quarters. Bake at 400° F. for about 35 to 40 minutes. While still hot, brush with butter.

Boston Brown Bread

1½ cups white flour
1½ teaspoons baking soda
1½ teaspoons salt
2 cups whole wheat flour
1 cup raisins, chopped or ground
½ cup sugar
½ cup molasses
1 egg
1¾ cups buttermilk

Put all ingredients in a mixing bowl in the order given. Beat together well. Fill greased No. 2 cans (20-ounce size) about two-thirds full. Cover with several thicknesses of waxed paper and tie securely. Place on a rack in steamer (rack should raise the cans 1 inch off the bottom). Steam for 3 hours. May also be baked for 45 minutes in oven heated to 350° F. Remove covers and bake 20 minutes more. (Baked variety is not quite as moist as the steamed.)

Homemade Corn Bread Mix

4 cups yellow cornmeal
4 cups white flour
¾ cup sugar
2 teaspoons salt
¼ cup baking powder
1 cup shortening

Sift cornmeal, flour, sugar, salt, and baking powder together 4 times. Cut shortening into sifted dry ingredients until mixture resembles fine crumbs. Store in a covered container at room temperature. Makes 10 cups of mix.

Corn Bread

Mix 2½ cups of the corn bread mix with one beaten egg and 1 cup of milk, stirring lightly until combined. Bake in a greased 8-inch square pan at 425° F. for 30 to 35 minutes.

Pancakes from Corn Bread Mix

Place 3 cups corn bread mix, 2 cups milk, and 1 egg in a mixing bowl. Beat about 1 minute with a rotary egg beater until batter is smooth. Do not overbeat. Bake on a hot, greased griddle. Makes 16 to 18 pancakes.

Never-Stir Bran Muffins

2 cups boiling water
5 teaspoons baking soda
4 cups All Bran cereal
2 cups 40% Bran Flakes cereal
2 cups chopped dates or raisins
1 cup chopped nuts
1 cup shortening
2 cups sugar
4 eggs
1 quart buttermilk (fresh or reconstituted powdered)
5 cups flour
1 teaspoon salt

Stir the baking soda into the boiling water and set aside. In a *very large* bowl place the cereals, dates or raisins, and nuts; set aside. In a large mixing bowl cream the sugar and shortening together. Beat in the eggs one at a time. Stir in the buttermilk, flour, and salt. Pour the soda-water mixture in and mix well. Finally, pour the batter over the cereal mixture and blend well. Store in an airtight container in the refrigerator and use as needed. (Mixture will keep for up to 6 weeks.) Never stir again after it has been mixed. To bake, fill greased muffin tins two-thirds full and bake at 375° F. for about 20 minutes. Makes 5 dozen muffins.

Whole Wheat Banana Bread

¼ cup margarine
1¼ cups brown sugar, packed
2 eggs
2 tablespoons milk
½ teaspoon salt
1 teaspoon baking soda
2 cups whole wheat flour
1 cup ripe bananas, mashed
½ cup chopped nuts

In a large mixing bowl, mix margarine, brown sugar, eggs, and milk until creamy. Add remaining ingredients and stir until well combined. Pour into a well-greased loaf pan. Bake at 350° F. for 45 minutes. Remove from pan and let cool on rack.

Coconut Bread

4 eggs
2 cups sugar
1 cup oil
1 teaspoon coconut flavoring
3 cups flour
½ teaspoon baking soda
½ teaspoon baking powder
½ teaspoon salt
1 cup buttermilk
1 cup chopped walnuts or pecans
1 cup shredded coconut
1 cup sugar
½ cup water
2 tablespoons butter
1 teaspoon coconut flavoring

In a large mixing bowl, beat eggs. Add 2 cups sugar, oil, and 1 teaspoon flavoring and blend well. Sift dry ingredients together and add to egg mixture alternately with buttermilk. Mix thoroughly. Add nuts and coconut. Pour into 2 greased and floured 3½" x 7½" loaf tins. Bake at 325° F. for 1¼ hours. Combine the 1 cup sugar, water, and butter in a saucepan and boil for 5 minutes. Add coconut flavoring and pour over hot bread. Let bread stand for several hours or overnight before serving.

Ginger Loaf

½ cup shortening
1 cup sugar
1 egg
1 cup milk
½ cup molasses
1 teaspoon baking soda
2½ cups flour, stirred and measured
1 teaspoon cinnamon
1 teaspoon baking powder
½ teaspoon ginger
¼ teaspoon salt
Pinch of cloves

In a large mixing bowl, cream together shortening and sugar. Stir in egg and milk. Add molasses and baking soda, and blend. Sift together remaining ingredients and add to shortening mixture; beat 3 minutes. Pour into a well-greased loaf pan. Bake at 350° F. for 1 hour or until bread springs back at touch. Remove from pan and cool on a rack. Delicious with party meats or spread with cream cheese and chives.

Orange Pecan Loaf

⅔ cup fresh orange juice
3 tablespoons (3 oranges) grated orange peel
3 tablespoons butter or margarine, melted
½ cup finely cut dates
½ cup chopped pecans
1 cup minus 2 tablespoons sugar
1 egg, slightly beaten
2 cups sifted flour
1 teaspoon baking powder
½ teaspoon baking soda
½ teaspoon salt

In a large mixing bowl, combine orange juice, orange peel, dates, butter, nuts, sugar, and egg. Sift dry ingredients and add to creamed mixture all at once; stir until flour is moistened. Turn into a greased loaf pan. Bake at 350° F. for 1 hour or until done. Remove from pan and cool on a rack. Flavor improves if bread is allowed to age overnight, wrapped tightly in plastic wrap.

Poppy Seed Bread

2 eggs
1½ cups sugar
¾ cup oil
1 teaspoon vanilla
½ cup poppy seeds
2 cups flour, stirred and measured
1 teaspoon baking powder
1 teaspoon salt
1 cup evaporated milk

In a large mixing bowl, beat eggs; add sugar and oil, mixing well. Add vanilla and poppy seeds. Sift together dry ingredients and add to egg mixture alternately with milk. Spoon into a greased loaf pan. Bake at 375° F. for 50 minutes, or until done. Remove from pan and cool on a rack.

Whole Wheat Pancakes

¾ cup wheat (<u>not</u> flour)
1 cup water
1 cup milk
2 tablespoons oil
3 eggs, separated
1 tablespoon honey or sugar
½ teaspoon salt

Bring to a boil the wheat and water. Remove from heat and let sit overnight. Next morning, drain off excess water. Put drained wheat into blender. Add milk and blend until mixture is as thick as cream. Blend in oil, egg yolks, honey, and salt. Beat egg whites until stiff, and fold into batter. Cook as for pancakes. Serves 4 to 6.

Cheesy Hotcakes

1½ cups sifted whole wheat flour
1 tablespoon baking powder
¾ teaspoon salt
3 tablespoons honey
2 egg yolks
1½ cups milk
3 tablespoons oil
2 egg whites, beaten stiff
Shredded cheese

Combine flour, baking powder, and salt. Add honey, egg yolks, milk, and oil, and mix well. Fold in egg whites. Drop on lightly greased griddle. While the first side bakes, sprinkle tops with shredded cheese. Flip the cakes to finish cooking. Serve with chopped fresh or frozen fruit, sour cream and honey, or your favorite topping. Makes about 4 to 6 servings.

Perfect Pancakes

2 cups flour
4 teaspoons baking powder
½ teaspoon salt
2 tablespoons sugar
2 eggs, beaten
1¾ cups milk
3 tablespoons butter, melted

Sift dry ingredients together. Beat eggs in a mixing bowl and add milk and butter. Stir in dry ingredients and mix only until wet. Heat griddle until a drop of water dances on it. Ladle batter on griddle and cook until rim of each cake is full of broken bubbles and underside is golden brown. Turn over and brown other side. Makes 4 to 6 servings.

Cream Topping for Hotcakes

2 tablespoons cornstarch
2 tablespoons flour
½ cup brown sugar, packed
Sprinkle of salt
½ cup cold milk
2 cups milk
½ teaspoon vanilla
2 tablespoons butter

Mix together the cornstarch, flour, brown sugar, salt, and ½ cup cold milk. Scald the 2 cups milk and stir in the sugar-flour mixture; continue cooking and stirring until the mixture bubbles and thickens. Add vanilla and butter. Serve hot over pancakes. Topping may also be topped with fresh berries or other fruit. Leftover topping may be stored in the refrigerator and used later as a pudding or pie filling. Serves 4.

Wheat Waffles

1 cup milk
1 cup whole wheat (<u>not</u> flour)
½ cup milk
4 teaspoons baking powder
½ cup oil
3 eggs
½ teaspoon salt

In blender, mix milk and wheat at high speed for 2 minutes. Continue blending as you add milk, baking powder, oil, eggs, and salt. Bake in waffle iron and serve with your favorite toppings. Batter can also be used for pancakes.

Variations

1. Place paper-thin slices of ham on waffle grids before pouring batter.

2. Place broken pecans on grids and pour batter over.

Belgian Waffles

1 package yellow cake mix
1 cup heavy cream
4 eggs, separated
½ teaspoon salt

Beat the cake mix, cream, egg yolks, and salt for 2 minutes at medium speed. Beat egg whites until stiff and gently fold into batter. Bake in waffle iron until golden brown. Top with sliced strawberries, powdered sugar, and whipped cream.

Sopapillas

2 cups flour
¼ cup instant dry milk
2 teaspoons baking powder
1 teaspoon salt
1 tablespoon lard or shortening
¾ cup water

Mix all ingredients together and knead to make elastic dough. Roll very thin. Cut in 2- to 3-inch squares. Fry in deep fat heated to 365° F. Squares blow up like little golden pillows. They are delicious served with honey butter. Serves 8 to 10.

German Pancakes

2 tablespoons butter
1 cup milk
1 cup eggs (about 4 large eggs)
1 cup flour

Heat a large ovenproof pan (a 10- or 12-inch cast-iron skillet is best) in oven set at 425° F. Drop the butter in and allow to melt. Put the milk, eggs, and flour in blender in the order given and whip on high speed until well blended and fluffy. Pour into the hot buttery pan and return quickly to the oven for 15 to 20 minutes. Cut into wedges and serve immediately with a variety of toppings: lemon juice and powdered sugar; sour cream and raspberry jam; butter or whipped cream and blueberry pie filling; whipped honey butter; honey; or syrup. Pancakes are also delicious served with roast beef. Serves 4 to 6.

SANDWICHES

Tuna Burgers

1 can (7 ounces) tuna
1 cup chopped celery
1 small onion, minced
½ cup diced processed yellow cheese
¼ cup mayonnaise
Salt and pepper to taste
6 hamburger buns

Combine all ingredients except buns and mix well. Fill buns with tuna mixture. Wrap buns in foil. (Can be refrigerated at this point.) Bake at 350° F. for 20 to 25 minutes, or heat on grill. Sandwiches can also be made open faced, using 3 buns; broil until cheese melts.

Red Devil

1 tablespoon butter
1 small onion, chopped
1 can (10 ounces) condensed tomato soup
1 cup sharp Cheddar cheese, cut fine
2 teaspoons Worcestershire sauce
1 teaspoon prepared mustard
Cayenne pepper to taste
1 egg, beaten
8 slices buttered toast or English muffins

Melt butter in double boiler. Add all other ingredients except toast. Stir and heat until cheese is melted and well blended. Spread on hot toast. Serves 8.

Lemon-Pepper Sandwich Loaf

1 loaf (16 ounces) unsliced white bread
½ cup lemon-pepper butter (below), softened
1 tablespoon prepared mustard
2 teaspoons poppy seeds
8 slices (8 ounces) process Swiss cheese
8 strips bacon, cooked, drained, and crumbled

Cut the bread into nine slices, cutting to but not through the bottom crust. Combine lemon butter, mustard, and poppy seeds; mix well. Set aside 3 tablespoons of mixture. Spread remainder on all cut surfaces of bread. Place one slice of cheese in each cut; sprinkle bacon over cheese. Spread reserved lemon-pepper butter mixture on top and sides of loaf. Bake on ungreased baking sheet at 350° F. for 15 to 20 minutes.

Lemon-Pepper Butter

1 pound butter
½ cup snipped chives (fresh or dried)
1½ teaspoons grated lemon peel
2 tablespoons lemon juice
½ teaspoon freshly ground black pepper

In a small mixer bowl, cream butter until light and fluffy. Add remaining ingredients and mix thoroughly to blend well. Store in refrigerator in a tightly covered container until needed, or freeze in ice cube trays and use one block at a time for spinach, fish, or other dishes. Makes 2 cups.

Note: Use this seasoned butter to add flavor to vegetables, or brush over broiled fish, beefsteaks, or pork cutlets. Spread it on toast, English muffins, or dinner rolls for the beginning of a tasty hot sandwich. Melt it to use as a dip for shrimp, lobster, or artichokes.

Stromboli

1 loaf French bread
1 pound bulk sausage
1 large Spanish onion, sliced
Monterey Jack or Swiss cheese slices

Cut bread horizontally so that bottom section is thicker than top. Scoop out insides with spoon and save for crumbs or bread pudding. Crumble and sauté sausage with onion until meat is cooked and onion is limp. Drain off excess fat. Fill bread cavity with meat and onions. Place cheese slices on meat and cover with bread top. Slice into serving pieces; assemble loaf on foil and wrap securely. (Can be refrigerated at this point.) Bake at 400° F. for 30 minutes or until cheese has melted and run down through meat. No seasoning is necessary. Serve with dill pickle spears. Serves 4 to 6.

Texas Burgers

1 pound ground beef
1 cup bread crumbs
1 egg, beaten
½ cup catsup
1 cup grated Cheddar cheese
¼ cup diced green pepper (optional)
2 tablespoons minced onion
¼ cup lemon juice
½ teaspoon pepper
1 teaspoon salt
8 slices bacon
8 sesame hamburger buns

Combine all ingredients except bacon and buns and shape into 8 patties. Wrap 1 slice bacon around each patty and secure with toothpicks. (May be refrigerated at this point.) Bake in a shallow pan at 400° F. for 45 minutes. Serve on sesame buns. Serves 8.

Guacamole Burgers

1 pound ground beef
½ cup corn chips, crushed
⅓ cup milk
1 teaspoon Worcestershire sauce
½ teaspoon onion salt
Avocado slices
Tomato slices
Shredded lettuce
6 sesame hamburger buns

Mix together ground beef, corn chips, milk, Worcestershire sauce, and onion salt; shape into

6 patties. Grill 6 to 7 minutes on each side. Top with avocado and tomato slices and shredded lettuce. Serve on toasted sesame buns. Serves 6.

Steak and Everything

1 medium onion, sliced thin
1 pound lean beef, sliced thin across the grain
6 to 8 mushrooms, sliced
1 tomato, chopped
½ green pepper, sliced (optional)
¼ pound shredded cheese (or more to taste)
Lemon pepper
4 sourdough rolls or favorite sandwich buns

Sauté the onion in a little butter until it is just transparent. Remove from pan and set aside. Add beef to butter in pan and stir-fry over medium heat until it browns. Stir in the onions, mushrooms, tomato, pepper, cheese, and a sprinkle of lemon pepper. Serve on hot toasted rolls. Serves 4.

If you deal generously with others, though they be selfish and unjust, they will make an exception in your favor and deal truly with you.

Open-faced Danish Sandwich

Thinly sliced dark bread
Butter
Slices of meat, such as smoked salmon, roast beef, or ham
Capers
Hard-boiled eggs, sliced
Olives
Pickles
Dill sprigs
Parsley
Watercress
Sprouts

For each open-face sandwich, spread a slice of bread thickly with the butter. Arrange a slice of meat on the bread and garnish with any or all of remaining ingredients. Use your imagination; the possibilities are endless.

Gourmet Gambler

12 slices bacon
1 can (8 ounces) mushroom stems and pieces
1 jar (6 ounces) marinated artichoke hearts
1 tablespoon butter
¼ teaspoon salt
¼ teaspoon pepper
6 hamburger buns or English muffins
Mayonnaise or salad dressing
6 slices Cheddar cheese
Lettuce leaves
Tomato slices

Cook bacon until crisp. Drain on paper towels. Crumble coarsely six slices of the bacon. Set remaining slices of bacon aside. Sauté mushrooms and artichoke hearts in the butter. Add salt, pepper, and the crumbled bacon. Butter and toast buns. Spread buns with mayonnaise or salad dressing to taste. Spoon mushroom mixture on bottom half of each bun and top with a slice of Cheddar cheese. Broil until bubbly. Place remaining cooked bacon slices over cheese. Add lettuce leaves and tomato slices, and cover with top of bun. Serve hot. Serves 6.

Rocky Mountain Special

½ pound sharp Cheddar cheese, diced small
1 tablespoon butter
½ teaspoon dry mustard
Cayenne pepper to taste
1 egg, slightly beaten
½ cup apple cider or juice
4 slices toast

Combine cheese, butter, mustard, and cayenne pepper in a heavy-bottomed pan. Cook over low heat, stirring constantly, until the cheese has melted. Beat a little of the hot cheese mixture into the egg. Then return the egg-cheese mixture to the pan and add salt to taste. Add the cider and cook 1 to 2 minutes more. Spoon over toast. Makes 4 open-face sandwiches.

Variations

Rocky Mountain Club Special: Cook 8 broccoli spears in boiling salted water until just tender (about 5 minutes). In a skillet, fry 8 slices Canadian bacon in a little butter. Make 1 recipe of the Rocky Mountain Special sauce (above). Butter 4 slices of bread. On each slice place 2 slices Canadian bacon, 2 slices cooked turkey breast, and 2 broccoli spears. Cover with a generous portion of sauce and sprinkle with sesame seeds. Makes 4 servings.

Ham and Asparagus Special: On each slice of buttered bread, place 2 slices cooked ham and 2 asparagus spears. Top with Rocky Mountain Special sauce.

Health Sandwich

1 cup shredded lettuce
1 cup fresh bean sprouts
1 cup grated Cheddar cheese
¾ cup grated carrot
½ cup raisins
½ cup chopped walnuts
4 slices whole-grain bread
2½ tablespoons honey
2½ tablespoons lemon juice
1 cup plain yogurt
½ cup alfalfa sprouts

Toss the lettuce, bean sprouts, cheese, carrot, raisins, and walnuts together; spoon onto the bread. Combine honey, lemon juice, and yogurt and blend until smooth. Spoon the dressing over the vegetables and sprinkle alfalfa sprouts on top. Serves 4. Filling can also be served in pita bread.

Basque Omelet Sandwiches

6 French rolls
½ pound sliced cooked ham
2 tablespoons salad oil
1 green pepper, chopped
1 medium onion, chopped
1 clove garlic, minced
1 medium tomato, peeled, seeded, and chopped
7 eggs
Salt and pepper
½ pound Monterey Jack cheese, sliced

Cut each roll in half lengthwise and scoop out most of the inside (save for other uses). Cover

the bottom half of each roll with a slice of ham. In a 10-inch frying pan heat 2 tablespoons oil over medium heat. Add green pepper, onion, garlic, and tomato; cook, stirring constantly, until tender-crisp. Beat the eggs slightly. Stir into sautéed vegetables and add salt and pepper to taste. Reduce heat to medium low and stir gently until eggs are softly scrambled. Spoon cooked egg-vegetable mixture over ham on each roll. Place a slice of cheese in scooped-out top of each roll, and cover the sandwich filling in the roll bottom. Wrap each roll in foil. (refrigerated at this point.) Heat wrap   ches at 375° F. for 15 to 20 minutes (tes if they have been refrigerated

Savory Pork Her

1 can (8 ounces) tomato sau
⅓ cup chili sauce
3 tablespoons brown sugar
1 clove garlic, minced
½ cup sliced pimiento-st
1 tablespoon Worcester
½ pound thinly sliced
Sauerkraut or lettuce
4 pumpernickel rolls

In a saucepan, combine tomato sauce, chili sauce, brown sugar, garlic, olives, and Worcestershire sauce; simmer for 5 minutes. Add pork slices and heat. To assemble the sandwiches, layer hot pork mixture and sauerkraut or shredded lettuce on buns. Serves 4.

Flatbread Sandwiches

Flatbread (also called pocket bread or pita) can be found in most supermarkets today. Pita is good hot or cold with such fillings as cheese, bean sprouts, avocado, olives, chopped onion, alfalfa sprouts, chopped tomato, sour cream, various meats, and lettuce. Here are some suggestions.

Ham and Cheese Pita: Slit open the side of the pita and spread the inside with soft butter. Stuff in slices of ham alternately with slices of cheese and pickle. Place under the broiler and toast one side until warm. Turn pita over. Brush top with a little egg glaze and sprinkle with sesame seeds. Toast until just light brown.

Lamb-filled Pita: Save some lamb and a little juice from your next roast. Stuff pita with 3 or 4 slices of warm cooked lamb, moistened with juice or gravy.

Corned Beef Pita: Fill pita with 3 to 5 slices cooked corned beef brushed with mustard. Toast, if desired. This is particularly good with whole wheat pita.

Crabmeat Special on English Muffins

6 ounces crabmeat, canned or fresh
3 tablespoons mayonnaise
1 tablespoon fresh lemon juice, or to taste
Salt to taste
Freshly ground pepper
2 English muffins
Butter to taste
1 large tomato, sliced thin
4 slices Swiss cheese

Drain the crabmeat and toss with mayonnaise, lemon juice, salt, and pepper. Split and toast the muffins and butter them while they are warm. Spread crabmeat evenly over each muffin half; cover with a tomato slice, and top with a slice of cheese. Broil until the cheese is bubbly. Serves 2.

A true friend unblossoms freely, advises justly, assists readily, adventures wildly, takes one patiently, defends courageously, and continues a friend unchangeably. (William Penn)

Pecan-Cheese Spread

2 packages (3 ounces each) cream cheese
½ pound Cheddar cheese, shredded
½ cup pecans or walnuts, chopped
Garlic salt to flavor
Paprika

Let cream cheese soften at room temperature. Mix in the Cheddar cheese, nuts, and garlic salt. Shape into two long rolls and roll in paprika. Store in refrigerator and use as sandwich spread when needed. Makes 10 to 12 sandwiches.

The Golden Rule contains no inches or feet, yet it is the standard measurement of all mankind. (G.L. Herbstreet)

Pimiento Cheese Spread

2 tablespoons flour
Salt to taste
1 teaspoon prepared mustard
1 egg, beaten
⅓ cup sugar
⅓ cup vinegar
¾ cup water
1 pound Velveeta cheese, chopped
1 small can pimiento, diced

Mix flour, salt, and mustard with enough water to make it the consistency of thick cream. Place in the top of a double boiler and add egg, sugar, vinegar, and water. Bring to a boil. Remove from heat and add cheese and pimiento. Mix well and cool. Use for sandwiches, as a spread for crackers, or to stuff celery. If desired, add chopped green olives. Yield: 1 quart.

A potful of love-
spread it around

Soups and Chili

SOUPS

Quick Homemade Vegetable Soup

4 cups tomato juice or stewed tomatoes
5 cups beef bouillon
½ head cabbage, finely chopped
2 or 3 zucchini, sliced
6 or 7 carrots, sliced
2 or 3 potatoes, diced
4 tablespoons dry onion
1 pound green beans (optional)
Fresh mushrooms
1 pound ground beef
Garlic powder to taste
Salt and pepper to taste
1 teaspoon Italian seasoning (optional)

Combine in a large kettle all the liquid and vegetables. Brown ground beef with seasonings and add to soup. Simmer until vegetables are tender. Serve immediately, or refrigerate and reheat later. Serves 10 to 12.

Jack Sprat Soup

½ head cabbage, finely chopped
1 can or 3 cups fresh bean sprouts
1 can (20 ounces) French-cut green beans
6 ribs celery, diced
8 cups water
4 cups tomatoes or tomato juice
¼ cup dried onion flakes
12 beef bouillon cubes
1 clove garlic, finely diced
1 bay leaf
½ teaspoon basil
1 tablespoon chopped parsley

Place all ingredients in a large pot and simmer, covered, at least 1 hour. Serves 10 to 12. This soup has few calories, but it is nourishing and filling. It also improves in flavor each time it is reheated.

Variation
Cut up 1 pound frankfurters and add to simmering soup.

Minestrone

4 cups canned tomatoes
4 cups water
1 can (10 ounces) consommé
1 small can (8 ounces) tomato sauce
4 large ribs celery, diced
3 large carrots, diced
2 large onions, chopped
1 teaspoon basil
½ teaspoon oregano
1 tablespoon parsley
1 or 2 cloves garlic
1 tablespoon sugar
1 pound bulk sausage
1 can (10 ounces) green beans
1 can (16 ounces) kidney beans
1 cup elbow macaroni (uncooked)
Salt and pepper to taste

Put tomatoes, water, consommé, and tomato sauce in large soup pot. Add diced celery, carrots, and onions. Stir in basil, oregano, parsley, garlic, and sugar. In a separate frying pan, brown sausage; drain, and add to soup. Simmer very slowly for 5 hours. Add beans and macaroni and simmer for 1 more hour or until macaroni is tender. Add salt and pepper to taste. Serves 12.

Old-fashioned Potato Soup

6 medium potatoes, diced
3 large onions, chopped
1 teaspoon salt
1 can (15 ounces) evaporated milk
2 tablespoons butter
2 tablespoons chopped parsley
¼ cup shredded cheese

Cover potatoes and onions with water and cook in saucepan with salt until very tender, almost mushy. Add milk, butter, and parsley. Ladle into bowls; top with shredded cheese. This soup can be cooked in 5 minutes in a pressure cooker. Serves 6.

German Potato Soup

4 strips lean bacon, diced
6 leeks, sliced thin
¼ cup chopped onion
2 tablespoons flour
4 cups beef bouillon
3 large potatoes, sliced thin
2 egg yolks, beaten
1 cup sour cream
1 tablespoon minced parsley
¼ cup butter
Thinly sliced rolls

In a Dutch oven or deep saucepan, sauté bacon for 5 minutes. Add leeks and onion and sauté for 5 minutes. Stir in flour. Add bouillon slowly, stirring constantly. Add potatoes and simmer, covered, for 1 hour. Combine egg yolks and sour cream and stir into soup. Simmer for 10 minutes, stirring constantly. Add parsley. In a skillet, melt butter and cook slowly until it is rich brown. Sauté slices of roll in butter until brown and hot. Serve with soup. Serves 6.

Cream of Spinach Soup

1 pound fresh spinach, finely chopped
2 cans (10 ounces each) consommé
1 cup half-and-half
Salt and pepper to taste

Boil together the spinach and consommé until spinach is tender. Add the half-and-half and seasonings and heat through (do not boil). Serves 6.

Corn Chowder

2 slices bacon
4 cups milk
2 cups canned or frozen whole kernel corn, drained
2 cans (10 ounces each) cream of potato soup

Fry bacon until crisp and break into pieces. Set aside. In a large saucepan, combine the rest of the ingredients. Cover, and heat slowly, stirring occasionally, until soup reaches the simmer point. Top each serving with bacon bits. Serves 6 to 8.

Double-rich Corn Soup

2 tablespoons butter
3 tablespoons minced onion
⅓ cup minced celery with leaves
3 tablespoons flour
4 cups milk
1 can (16 ounces) cream-style corn
2½ teaspoons salt
⅛ teaspoon black pepper
3 tablespoons minced parsley or chives
Worcestershire sauce or meat sauce to taste (optional)

Over medium heat, sauté onion and celery in butter until tender. Blend in the flour. Add milk, and, stirring constantly, heat until smooth and thickened. Stir in the remaining ingredients. Heat and serve. Serves 6.

Variations

Diced cooked potatoes may be added. Or sprinkle crisp crumbled bacon on top of each serving.

Carrot Cream Soup

1 pound carrots, peeled and sliced
2 ribs celery, chopped
1 large onion, chopped
1 tablespoon oil
2 tablespoons butter
3 cups chicken or beef stock
½ bay leaf
Grated rind and juice of ½ orange
1 tablespoon lemon juice
Salt and pepper to taste
⅔ cup cream or evaporated milk
Chives

Sauté carrots, celery, and onions in oil and butter for 5 to 10 minutes. Add remaining ingredients except cream and chives. Bring to a boil, cover, and simmer 25 to 30 minutes. Remove the bay leaf and press soup through a sieve or whir in a blender until smooth. Return to pan, add cream, and heat. Adjust seasonings and serve, garnished with chives. This soup is quick and easy and can also be made a day ahead and reheated. Serves 6 to 8.

French Onion Soup

4 large onions, sliced thin
2 tablespoons butter
1 package dry onion soup mix

Sauté onions in butter until transparent and tender, stirring frequently. Add more butter if needed to keep them moist while cooking. Make onion soup according to package directions. Add the cooked onions. Serve hot. Serves 4 to 6.

Variations

1. Float a slice of toasted sourdough bread topped with shredded cheese in each bowl. If desired, place under broiler until cheese is melted.
2. Break 1 egg into each bowl, and spoon soup over egg until egg is cooked.
3. Sprinkle soup lightly with cayenne pepper.

Mushroom Soup

1 medium onion, chopped
¼ cup butter
½ pound fresh mushrooms, sliced
1 tablespoon chopped parsley
1 teaspoon salt
Pepper to taste
1 tablespoon lemon juice
¼ cup flour
6 cups water
1 cup cream or evaporated milk

Fry onion in butter until transparent. Add mushrooms, parsley, salt, pepper, and lemon juice. Cover and simmer until mushrooms are soft. Combine flour with 1 cup of the water; stir into mushroom mixture. Add remaining 5 cups water. Simmer 20 minutes. Just before serving, stir in the cream. Heat through, but do not boil. Serves 6 to 8.

Variations

1. Add a dollop of sour cream to each serving.
2. Add 1 pound thinly sliced beef, lightly browned in butter, and 1 pound broccoli, thinly sliced and cooked until tender.

Cream of Pumpkin Soup

1 medium onion, sliced
9 cups pumpkin or winter squash,
  peeled and chopped
¼ cup butter
2½ cups chicken stock
2½ cups milk
Salt and pepper to taste
¼ teaspoon grated nutmeg
½ cup cream
2 tablespoons parsley, chopped
Salted sunflower seeds

Fry onions and pumpkin or squash in the butter in a large pan for 5 minutes. Add stock and bring to a boil. Cover and simmer for about 1 hour, or until tender. Put in batches in blender and blend until smooth. Return to pan. Add milk and bring to a boil, whisking continuously. Simmer for 5 minutes. Add seasonings and cream. To serve, sprinkle each serving with parsley and sunflower seeds. Serves 10 to 12.

Clam Chowder

4 slices bacon, diced
2 cups potatoes, diced
1 cup celery, diced
1 cup onions, diced
Water
8 cups milk
2 cans (6½ ounces each) clams and juice
¾ cup flour
½ cup (1 square) butter, melted
Salt and pepper to taste
½ teaspoon dried basil
⅛ teaspoon paprika
¼ teaspoon mace (optional)
2 tablespoons minced parsley

Cook diced bacon in a soup pot until fat is rendered but bacon is not crisp. Remove from fat and set aside. Add vegetables to bacon fat; stir-fry a few minutes. Add water just to cover vegetables and simmer until potatoes are tender. Add milk and clams with juice. Blend flour into melted butter and then stir into hot soup. Add reserved bacon, salt and pepper, basil, paprika, and mace; simmer 10 minutes. Sprinkle parsley on top and serve. Serves 10 to 12.

Swiss Broccoli Soup

2 tablespoons butter
1 cup cooked cubed ham
1 cup water
1 package (10 ounces) frozen chopped broccoli
2 cups milk
3 tablespoons flour
½ teaspoon salt
Dash of pepper
2 cups shredded Swiss cheese

In a heavy kettle melt butter; add ham and brown lightly, stirring. Add 1 cup water and bring to a boil; add frozen broccoli and cook, covered, five minutes. In a small bowl combine milk and flour; blend until smooth. Add to ham mixture and cook until thick and smooth, stirring constantly. Add salt and pepper. Pour into individual soup bowls. Serve hot topped with shredded Swiss cheese. Serves 4 to 6.

Wash-day Bean Soup

1 pound small white beans
Water
1 small onion, chopped
2 cloves garlic, minced
Salt and pepper to taste
1 pound ground beef
4 cups or 1 can (30 ounces) tomatoes

Cook beans until tender in enough water to cover. Add onion, garlic, and salt and pepper. Brown meat and add to beans. Add tomatoes and simmer 10 minutes. Serves 8 to 10.

Split Pea and Mushroom Soup

8 cups water
1 pound split peas
2 ham hocks
1 cup chopped onion
1 cup shredded carrots
1 bay leaf
1½ teaspoons salt
¼ teaspoon pepper
½ pound fresh mushrooms, sliced
2 tablespoons butter

Place all ingredients except half of the mushrooms and the butter in a large kettle. Bring to boil; reduce heat and simmer until peas are tender, about 1½ hours. Remove ham hocks, cut meat off bone, and return meat to soup. Fry remaining half of mushrooms in 2 tablespoons butter for 3 minutes. Add to soup, and sprinkle with minced parsley. If desired, add a little milk, cream, or evaporated milk. Serve with croutons. This soup can be made ahead and rewarmed. Serves 10 to 12.

Lentil Soup

4 strips bacon, diced
2 medium onions, chopped
2 medium carrots, sliced
1 cup celery, sliced
8 cups hot water
2 cups cooked cubed ham (or more to taste)
1 package (16 ounces) lentils
1 teaspoon salt
½ teaspoon thyme leaves
2 bay leaves
Salt to taste
½ teaspoon pepper
2 tablespoons lemon juice

In a 5-quart Dutch oven or saucepan, fry bacon until crisp. Add onions, carrots, and celery and sauté until tender-crisp. Add the rest of the ingredients except the lemon juice. Cover and simmer for 1 hour or until lentils are tender. Stir in lemon juice and serve. Serves 6 to 8.

Chili from Scratch

½ pound dried pinto beans
5 cups canned tomatoes
2 or 3 green peppers, chopped
1½ tablespoons salad oil
1½ cups chopped onions
2 cloves garlic, crushed
½ cup chopped parsley
2½ pounds ground beef
1 pound ground lean pork
2 tablespoons chili powder (or to taste)
2 tablespoons salt
1½ teaspoons pepper

1½ teaspoons cumin seed
1½ teaspoons monosodium glutamate (optional)

*Prepare beans:** Pick over the beans and remove any stones. Wash and drain beans in a sieve and place them in a large saucepan, Dutch oven, or pressure cooker. (Never fill pressure cooker more than three-fourths full when cooking beans.) Add 3 cups water for each cup dried beans and bring to a boil (not under pressure). Boil beans for exactly 2 minutes; then cover the pan and set aside for 1 hour. Drain and then cover the beans with water. Add 1 teaspoon salt and other flavoring ingredients, if desired, such as whole garlic cloves, sliced onion, sliced carrot, bay leaves, blanched salt pork, or olive oil. If cooking in saucepan or Dutch oven, cook until tender, about 90 minutes. If cooking in pressure cooker, bring the beans to full pressure and time for exactly 3 minutes. Let the pressure go down by itself (10 to 15 minutes). Uncover the pan and let beans steep for 20 to 30 minutes so they will settle themselves and absorb the flavors they were cooked with. They are now ready to use.

Make chili: Add tomatoes to beans and simmer 5 minutes. Sauté green pepper in oil for 5 minutes; add onion and cook until tender, stirring constantly. Add garlic and parsley. Set aside. Sauté ground beef and ground pork together for 15 minutes; drain off excess fat. Combine meat and onion mixture and stir in chili powder; cook 10 minutes. Add to beans and stir in salt, pepper, cumin seed, and monosodium glutamate, if desired. Simmer, covered, for 1 hour. Cook uncovered for additional 30 minutes. Skim fat from top. (Can be refrigerated at this point.) Serves 12 to 15.

*This method of quick-soaking and cooking beans can be used for navy, great northern, black, pinto, red, and pea beans. Do not use it for flageolets, however, since they are too tender.

Pedernales Chili

4 pounds ground round
1 large onion, chopped
2 cloves garlic, minced
1 teaspoon oregano
1 teaspoon cumin
6 tablespoons chili powder (or to taste)

1½ cups canned whole tomatoes
2 dashes hot pepper sauce (or to taste)
Salt to taste
2 cups hot water

In a heavy skillet, brown ground round, onion, and garlic till onion is clear and all red has left meat. Drain off fat. Add remaining ingredients. Bring to boil; lower heat and simmer uncovered about 1 hour. Skim off fat during cooking. Serve Texas-style with a side dish of chili beans. Serves 10 to 12.

Quick Chili

1 pound lean ground beef
1 large onion, chopped
4 ribs celery, chopped
1 can (30 ounces) chili beans
4 cups tomatoes
1 can (10 ounces) condensed tomato soup
2 teaspoons sugar
Chili powder to taste
Salt to taste

Brown ground beef, onion, and celery until tender. Add remaining ingredients and bring to boil. Serve immediately or simmer as long as you wish. Flavor improves if chili is refrigerated overnight. Serves 8 to 10.

Gazpacho

6 to 8 medium tomatoes, peeled
1 medium onion, quartered
1 green pepper, cut in large pieces
1 cucumber, peeled
1 clove garlic
2 slices bread with crusts removed
½ teaspoon cumin
Salt and pepper to taste
Equal parts of vinegar and olive or vegetable oil (to taste)

Place in blender the tomatoes, onion, pepper, cucumber, and garlic; blend until smooth. Add bread, cumin, salt and pepper, vinegar, and oil. Blend well and serve in chilled bowls topped with fresh chopped tomatoes, onions, cucumbers, garlic croutons, and crisp crumbled bacon (optional). Serves 8 to 10.

Borscht

2 pounds lean beef, cut into 1½-inch chunks
Cooking oil
3 cups water
2 cups diced beets, drained
2 large onions, chopped
4 cups cabbage, coarsely chopped
3½ cups canned tomatoes
½ cup lemon juice
1 clove garlic, minced
¼ cup chopped parsley
1 bay leaf
½ teaspoon red pepper
3 tablespoons sugar
1 teaspoon salt
Freshly ground black pepper
Sour cream

Stir-fry the beef cubes in a little oil until brown. Add 3 cups water; cover and simmer for 1½ to 2 hours until tender. Add the beets, onions, cabbage, tomatoes, lemon juice, and seasonings; simmer for 1 hour. Serve hot or cold with sour cream or with Fancy Garnish.

Fancy Garnish

2 cups sour cream
1 clove garlic, finely minced
1 teaspoon salt
½ teaspoon freshly cracked black pepper
1 teaspoon grated lemon rind
¼ teaspoon sugar

Mix all ingredients together. Refrigerate.

Winning love once is not enough. Keep rewinning it. . . . In the last analysis it's up to you to save your marriage. (Hubert S. Howe)

Opportunity is often missed because we are broadcasting when we should be tuning in. (National Safety News)

My cup runneth over

Beverages, Hot and Cold

Beverages

BEVERAGES

Orange-Banana-Pineapple Punch

2 cans (12 ounces each) frozen orange juice, reconstituted
1 can (46 ounces) unsweetened pineapple juice
4 large bananas, mashed or mixed in the blender with part of juice

Combine all ingredients; freeze to a slush and serve as punch. May also be stored frozen solid. To serve, set out to partially thaw; then whip in blender or mash with potato masher. Serve plain as an ice or over a scoop of vanilla ice cream. This also makes a great appetizer served frozen with a sprig of mint.

Summer Punch

2 cups sugar
2 cups water
3 bananas, mashed
Juice of 3 oranges
Juice of 3 lemons
1 can (30 ounces) crushed pineapple
3 quarts carbonated lemon-lime beverage

Heat sugar and water together until dissolved. Cool. Add banana, fruit juices, and pineapple; freeze until slushy. Spoon slush into glasses and add lemon-lime beverage. Makes 30 servings (6-ounce servings).

Christmas Punch

1 quart vanilla ice cream
2½ quarts pineapple sherbert
2 cans (6 ounces each) frozen lemonade concentrate
1 can (6 ounces) frozen orange juice concentrate
9 cups cold water

Place all ingredients in a large container; whip together and serve. Serves 30 (6-ounce servings).

Orange/Almond Party Punch

2 cups sugar
2 cups water
2 cans (46 ounces each) orange juice
¾ cup fresh lemon juice
1 teaspoon vanilla
1 teaspoon almond extract
3 quarts carbonated lemon-lime beverage

Heat sugar and water until sugar is dissolved. Cool; add juices and flavorings. Add carbonated beverage. Makes 5 quarts.

Festive Punch

2 quarts cranberry juice cocktail
2 quarts pineapple juice
½ cup sugar
2 quarts ginger ale
1 orange, thinly sliced
1 lemon, thinly sliced

Combine juices and sugar in a punch bowl. Add ginger ale and enough ice to chill well. Float orange and lemon slices in punch. The juice and sugar syrup may be made ahead and refrigerated or frozen until ready to serve. Serves 36 (5-ounce servings).

Orange-Pineapple Party Punch

2 cans (46 ounces each) pineapple juice
2 cans (12 ounces each) frozen orange juice concentrate
¼ pound citric acid*
5 pounds sugar
5 gallons water

Mix all ingredients except water and store in refrigerator. When ready to serve, add water. It is inexpensive but tasty. Serves 100 (8-ounce servings) to 150 (6-ounce servings).

*Citric acid may be purchased at a drugstore.

Holiday Punch

2 quarts cranberry juice cocktail
1 can (6 ounces) frozen lemon juice concentrate
6 cans (6 ounces each) frozen pineapple juice concentrate
4 cans (6 ounces each) frozen orange juice concentrate
2 cans (6 ounces each) frozen grapefruit juice concentrate
4 cans (6 ounces each) frozen lemonade concentrate
3 quarts water
8 quarts ginger ale

Mix all ingredients but ginger ale in a glass or plastic container. (May be refrigerated at this point.) When ready to serve, pour into punch bowl and add ginger ale. Float an ice ring that has been made with pineapple chunks, strawberries, and mint leaves. Makes 4 gallons.

When you're in the right you can afford to keep your temper; when you're in the wrong you can't afford to lose it.

Oriental Punch

1 cup sugar
1 cup water
6 whole cloves
1-inch piece of stick cinnamon
½ tablespoon chopped fresh ginger (or 1 teaspoon ground ginger)
Fresh mint leaves, washed and crushed, or a drop of mint flavoring
Juice of 4 lemons
Juice of 4 large oranges

Boil sugar and water together for six minutes to make a syrup. Add cloves, cinnamon, ginger, and a handful of mint leaves. Cover and let steep about 1 hour; strain. Add fruit juices. (May be refrigerated at this point.) Pour into a punch bowl over crushed ice, and garnish with fresh mint leaves. Makes 12 servings.

Variation

Freeze in ice cream freezer for a delicious ice to serve as a cocktail or dessert.

Crowd-pleasing Punch

3 packages cherry-flavored unsweetened powdered drink mix
3 packages orange-flavored unsweetened powdered drink mix
6 cups sugar
1 can (46 ounces) pineapple juice
1 can (12 ounces) frozen lemonade concentrate

Mix all ingredients together to make the punch base. Store in refrigerator. When ready to use, mix 3 parts water to 1 part base. If desired, add ginger ale or other carbonated beverage. Mashed bananas may also be added. For a green punch, use 6 packages lemon-lime powdered drink mix. Makes enough base for 2 gallons punch.

Sangria

1 quart grape juice
1 quart carbonated lemon-lime beverage
3 cups orange juice
1 orange, thinly sliced
1 lime, thinly sliced

Mix juices and carbonated drink together in a large pitcher. Float slices of orange and lime on top. Add ice. Delicious served with Mexican or Spanish food. Serves 16 (5½-ounce servings).

Holiday Cocktail

6 eggs
¼ cup sugar
¼ teaspoon cinnamon
¼ teaspoon ginger
¼ teaspoon cloves
2 quarts orange juice
½ cup lemon juice
1 quart vanilla ice cream
1 quart ginger ale
Nutmeg

Beat eggs; stir in sugar, cinnamon, ginger, and cloves. Add orange juice and lemon juice. Refrigerate for 2 hours or longer. Add ice cream and ginger ale. Sprinkle with nutmeg. Serves 20 (6-ounce servings).

Mock Champagne

1 cup sugar
1 cup water
1 cup unsweetened grapefruit juice
½ cup orange juice
⅓ cup grenadine syrup
1 quart ginger ale

Bring sugar and water to boil, to dissolve sugar. Cool. Combine with juices and grenadine syrup. Chill. Add ginger ale just before serving. Makes 2 quarts, about 8 to 10 servings.

Pero Mocha

6 cups hot water
½ cup instant Pero
2 cups sugar (or to taste)
1 quart milk
2 pints whipping cream
1 gallon vanilla ice cream

Heat water to boiling and add Pero and sugar. Cool. Add milk, and store in refrigerator until ready to serve. Whip cream and add to cooled mixture. Add scoops of ice cream and serve. This may also be served with cookies as a dessert. Makes 7½ quarts.

A single grateful thought toward heaven is the most perfect prayer.

Yummy Hot Chocolate

8 squares unsweetened baking chocolate
2 tall cans evaporated milk
6 scant cups sugar
5 gallons water
Powdered milk to make 6 quarts
4 tall cans evaporated milk

Heat chocolate, 2 cans milk, and sugar together over low heat until sugar crystals are all dissolved. Whip together in a blender until smooth and thick. Heat 5 gallons of water to boiling and add powdered milk. Blend in 4 cans evaporated milk and the chocolate syrup. Makes 80 cups (8 ounces each). *Note:* Syrup can be stored in the refrigerator and used a spoonful at a time in a cup of hot milk.

Instant Cocoa Mix

16 cups (4 quarts) dry instant powdered milk
1 can (2 pounds) instant chocolate milk powder
1½ to 2 cups powdered sugar
1 jar (16 ounces) instant nondairy creamer

Combine all ingredients and store in a tightly covered container. To serve, fill cup ⅓ full of mix and add boiling water.

The future is that time when you'll wish you'd done what you aren't doing now! (Author unknown)

Forbidden fruits

Cakes, Cookies, Pies, and Other Desserts

Cakes

Cookies and Bars

Pies

Desserts

CAKES

...undt Cake

3 eggs
2 teaspoons vanilla
3 cups flour
1 teaspoon baking soda
1 teaspoon salt
1 teaspoon cinnamon
1 cup nuts, chopped
3 cups raw apples, peeled and chopped fine

Cream oil and sugar together. Add eggs and vanilla and beat until fluffy. Mix dry ingredients together and add to creamed mixture, blending thoroughly. Stir in nuts and apples. Pour into a well-greased Bundt pan and bake at 325° F. for 1 hour and 15 minutes. Cake is delicious served as is or with a frosting made of powdered sugar and cream cheese. Cake can also be baked in a 9" x 13" x 2" pan.

Banana Cake

2 cups sifted flour
¾ teaspoon salt
1⅓ cups sugar
1 teaspoon baking powder
1 teaspoon soda
½ cup butter or shortening
½ cup sour milk* or buttermilk
1 cup mashed bananas
2 eggs
1 teaspoon vanilla
½ cup chopped nuts

In a large mixing bowl, combine dry ingredients with the shortening and half the milk; beat for 2 minutes. Add the rest of the milk, bananas, eggs, and vanilla; beat for one minute. Stir in nuts. Turn batter into two 9-inch round cake pans or one 9" x 13" x 2" pan. Bake 25 minutes at 375° F. Cool on racks. Delicious frosted with whipped cream and sliced bananas or your favorite icing.

*To sour milk, add 1 tablespoon vinegar to ½ cup sweet milk.

Apricot Cake

2 cups canned apricots,* drained
2 teaspoons baking soda
2 teaspoons cinnamon
2 eggs
2 cups flour
1 cup sugar
½ teaspoon salt
1 cup oil
1 cup chopped nuts

Combine all ingredients in mixer bowl and beat 3 minutes. Bake in a greased Bundt pan at 350° F. for 45 to 50 minutes. Cake is delicious as is, sprinkled with powdered sugar, or frosted with the following icing:

½ cup butter
1 cup brown sugar
¼ cup evaporated milk
1¾ to 2 cups powdered sugar

Melt butter in a saucepan and add brown sugar. Place over medium heat and boil for 2 minutes. Carefully stir in milk and return to boil. Remove from heat and cool to lukewarm. Add powdered sugar and beat until of spreading consistency.

*Substitute any bottled fruit for apricots.

Carrot Cake

3 cups flour, sifted
1 cup white sugar
1 cup brown sugar
4 eggs
1½ cups oil
1 tablespoon baking powder
1 tablespoon baking soda
1 tablespoon cinnamon
½ teaspoon salt
2 jars (7½ ounces each) junior (baby food) carrots or 2 cups cooked mashed carrots
1 cup chopped walnuts

Mix all ingredients together. Spoon into an ungreased 10-inch tube pan and bake at 375° F. for 1 hour. Cool before removing from pan. Cake is very moist and keeps well.

Lazy Lady Cake

2 eggs
1 cup sugar
1 teaspoon vanilla
1 cup cake flour
1 teaspoon baking powder
¼ teaspoon salt
½ cup milk
2 tablespoons butter

Combine eggs, sugar, and vanilla and beat until thick and lemon colored. Add sifted dry ingredients. Heat milk and butter together to boiling. Add to flour mixture, beating until well blended. Bake in a buttered 8-inch square baking pan at 350° F. for 30 to 40 minutes. Remove from oven and frost while warm.

Lazy Lady Frosting

¾ cup brown sugar (packed)
½ cup melted butter
¼ cup cream
1 cup coconut

Combine all ingredients and blend well. Spread on cake and place under broiler for a few minutes until golden brown.

Butter Sponge Cake

1 cup butter or margarine
1 cup sugar
6 egg yolks
2 cups flour
½ teaspoon baking powder
½ teaspoon salt
6 egg whites
¾ cup sugar

Cream margarine and 1 cup sugar together until fluffy. Add egg yolks one at a time, beating well after each addition. Sift together flour, baking powder, and salt and stir into the creamed mixture. Beat the 6 egg whites until frothy; gradually add ¾ cup sugar, and beat until very stiff. Fold egg whites into butter-flour mixture. Grease the bottom of a 10-inch tube pan and pour batter in. Bake at 350° F. for 50 to 55 minutes. Invert to cool. Cake is delicious plain, sprinkled with powdered sugar, or served with fresh fruit and a dollop of whipped cream.

Variation

To make Poppy Seed Cake, fold ¼ cup poppy seeds into batter.

Pineapple Dream Cake

1 package lemon or yellow cake mix
1 cup brown sugar
1 can (20 ounces) crushed pineapple with juice
2 packages (3¾ ounces each) lemon or vanilla <u>instant</u> pudding mix
3 cups milk
1 large container (12 ounces) frozen dessert topping
½ cup sliced almonds, lightly toasted, or ½ cup flaked coconut

Prepare cake mix according to directions on package. Pour into an 11" x 17" x 2" baking pan, and bake at 350° F. for 15 to 20 minutes. Remove pan from oven. Combine sugar and pineapple, including juice, and bring to a full boil. Spoon pineapple evenly over hot cake. Cool. Combine pudding mix and milk; when set, spread over chilled cake. Spread with dessert topping. Cake can be served immediately but is best if made the day before serving and refrigerated. Just before serving, sprinkle nuts or coconut on top. Serves 20 to 30.

Date Pudding Cake

2 cups fruit cocktail, drained (reserve juice)
½ cup juice from fruit cocktail
2 cups sugar
2 eggs
¼ cup butter
2 teaspoons vanilla
2½ cups flour
2 teaspoons baking soda
1 teaspoon salt
½ cup chopped dates
1 cup chopped nuts
½ cup brown sugar
½ teaspoon cinnamon

In a large mixing bowl, combine fruit cocktail and ½ cup juice, sugar, eggs, butter, vanilla, flour, soda, and salt; beat for 2 minutes. Stir in dates and ½ cup of the nuts. Pour into a greased 9″ x 13″ x 2″ baking pan. Combine brown sugar, cinnamon, and remaining ½ cup nuts and sprinkle over batter. Bake at 350° F. (325° F. in glass baking dish) for 40 to 45 minutes. While cake bakes, prepare sauce:

**¾ cup sugar
½ cup evaporated milk
½ cup butter
1 teaspoon vanilla**

Combine ingredients in a small saucepan. Bring to a boil over medium heat and boil for 2 minutes. Pour over hot cake. Serve cake warm or cold with a dollop of whipped cream. Cake keeps very well and can be reheated in a warm oven. It is also delicious served with a hot lemon-butter sauce. Serves 12 to 18.

Write in your heart that every day is the best day of the year. Finish every day, and be done with it. You have done what you could. (Ralph Waldo Emerson)

Chocolate Tea Cakes

**1 egg
1 cup granulated sugar
½ cup cocoa
1 teaspoon vanilla
1½ cups sifted cake flour
1 teaspoon baking soda
½ teaspoon baking powder
½ teaspoon salt
½ cup cold water
½ cup shortening
½ cup boiling water**

Put all ingredients in a bowl in the order given, pouring hot water directly on the shortening. Beat on low speed until the batter is smooth (batter will be thin). Drop by spoonfuls into muffin tins lined with cupcake papers. Bake at 375° F. for 15 to 20 minutes. Makes 50 tiny tea cakes or 24 regular-size cupcakes.

Cinnamon Puffs

**1½ cups butter
1¼ cups sugar
3 eggs
3 cups flour
1 tablespoon baking powder
1½ teaspoons nutmeg
1¼ cups milk
1¼ cups sugar
2 to 3 tablespoons cinnamon (to taste)**

In a large mixing bowl, combine ¾ cup of the butter, sugar, eggs, flour, baking powder, nutmeg, and milk; beat until smooth. Place cupcake papers in muffin tins and fill ⅔ full. Bake at 350° F. for 15 minutes. While cupcakes are baking, combine sugar and cinnamon; set aside. Melt remaining ¾ cup of the butter. Remove cupcakes from oven and, while still hot, peel off paper. Roll cupcakes in melted butter and then in cinnamon-sugar. Makes 2 dozen large cupcakes or 5 dozen tea-cake size.

"A Cup of Each" Sponge Cake

**Eggs to make 1 cup
1 cup flour
1 cup sugar
Flavoring***

In mixing bowl place eggs, flour, and sugar. Beat on high speed until thick and lemon colored, about 5 to 10 minutes. Add desired flavoring. Pour into an ungreased 8-inch square pan and bake at 350° F. for about 30 minutes. Remove from pan and cool on a rack. Use for trifle or shortcake.

Note: You can use this recipe to make any size cake you wish. Just measure the eggs first and add equal amounts of flour and sugar. It is a good recipe for children to make, since they don't need to follow a recipe.

*Use any flavoring you desire. To make lemon cake, add 1 teaspoon grated rind and a few drops lemon flavoring.

Variations

1. Split cake horizontally. Spread favorite pie

filling over bottom half; replace top half, and cover with whipped cream.

2. While cake is baking, combine 1 cup powdered sugar and the juice of 1 lemon. Immediately after removing cake from oven (do not remove from pan), pour lemon glaze over

cake. Prick cake with a toothpick so lemon glaze will seep in. Serve warm with whipped cream.

3. Cut cake into strips. Frost thinly with strawberry or raspberry jam; then roll in chopped coconut.

COOKIES AND BARS

Outstanding Sugar Cookies

1 cup sugar
1 cup butter
1 egg
3 tablespoons cream
1 teaspoon vanilla
3 cups flour
1½ teaspoons baking powder
½ teaspoon salt

In a large mixing bowl, cream sugar and butter until fluffy. Add egg and mix thoroughly. Add cream and vanilla. Stir in dry ingredients. On a floured board, roll out the dough as thin as possible and cut with favorite shapes. Sprinkle with sugar and bake on an ungreased cookie sheet at 400° F. for 8 to 10 minutes. Watch closely and do not let them get brown. Makes 3 dozen cookies.

Coconut Macaroons

2 tablespoons cornstarch
3 cups shredded coconut
3 egg whites
1 cup sugar
1 teaspoon vanilla

Mix cornstarch and coconut together and set aside. In a mixing bowl, beat the egg whites until stiff but not dry. Gradually beat in the sugar. Fold in the coconut. Cook 15 minutes in a double boiler, stirring often. Remove from heat

and add vanilla. Drop by spoonfuls 1 inch apart onto greased cookie sheet. Bake at 300° F. for 20 to 25 minutes. Makes about 4 dozen.

Richest-Ever Chocolate Chip Cookies

2 cups butter or 1 cup each butter and margarine
3 eggs
2 cups sugar
2 cups brown sugar (packed)
1 teaspoon vanilla
6 cups flour
1½ teaspoons salt
1½ teaspoons baking soda
3 cups chocolate chips
1½ cups chopped nuts

Beat butter, eggs, sugars, and vanilla until light and creamy. Sift flour, salt, and baking soda together, and add to creamed mixture; blend thoroughly. Stir in chocolate chips and nuts. (Dough should be slightly crumbly.) Drop dough by large spoonfuls or from small ice cream scoop (1¾-inch size) onto a greased cookie sheet. Bake at 350° F. for 8 to 10 minutes or until cookies are light and look not quite done. *Don't overbake.* Remove from cookie sheet immediately and cool on racks. Makes about 80 large cookies. Cookies are delicious warmed in the microwave oven for a few seconds.

Date Pinwheel Cookies

2¼ cups chopped dates
1 cup sugar
1 cup water
1 cup chopped walnuts or pecans
1 cup shortening
2 cups brown sugar
3 eggs, beaten
1 teaspoon vanilla
4 cups sifted flour
1 teaspoon baking soda
1 teaspoon salt

In a saucepan, combine dates, sugar, and water and bring to a boil. Cook over low heat until thick. Add nuts and cool. In a large mixing bowl, cream shortening, brown sugar, eggs, and vanilla. Add flour, baking soda, and salt, and mix well. Chill dough. Divide dough in half and roll each half into a rectangle ¼-inch thick. Spread date filling on rectangles and roll as for jelly roll. Chill again (overnight, if possible). Cut into ½-inch slices and bake on a greased cookie sheet at 375° F. for 10 to 12 minutes. Makes 3 to 4 dozen cookies.

Ginger Cookies

¾ cup shortening
1 cup brown sugar
1 egg
¼ cup molasses
2¼ cups sifted flour
2 teaspoons baking soda
¼ teaspoon salt
¼ teaspoon cloves
1 teaspoon cinnamon
1 teaspoon ginger

In a large mixing bowl, beat shortening, brown sugar, egg, and molasses until creamy. Sift remaining ingredients together and combine with creamed mixture. Chill dough. Roll into balls about 1 inch in diameter and dip one side in sugar. Place balls sugar side up on a greased cookie sheet and bake at 350° F. for 12 to 15 minutes. For a crackly top, sprinkle a few drops of water on each cookie before baking. Makes 3 to 4 dozen cookies.

Extravagant Cookies

2 cups brown sugar
2 cups white sugar
2 cups butter (do not use margarine)
4 eggs
4 cups flour
1 teaspoon salt
2 teaspoons baking powder
2 teaspoons baking soda
5 cups rolled oats
2 teaspoons vanilla
3 cups walnuts, chopped
2 chocolate candy bars (8 ounces each), chopped coarsely, or 3 packages (6 ounces each) chocolate chips, or 2 cups raisins

Cream sugars and butter; add eggs and beat well. Sift flour, salt, baking powder, and baking soda together; add to creamed mixture with oats, vanilla, walnuts, and chocolate or raisins; mix well. Mold into balls about the size of a golf ball and place on a greased cookie sheet 2 inches apart. Press down to flatten slightly. Bake at 400° F. for 6 to 8 minutes. Do not overbake! Let cool before removing from pan. Makes 6 dozen cookies.

Cherry Delights

1 cup sugar
¾ cup shortening
1 egg
1 teaspoon vanilla
2¼ cups flour
½ teaspoon salt
½ teaspoon baking soda
½ teaspoon baking powder
1 cup chopped dates
1 cup chopped pecans
2 cups cornflake crumbs
⅓ cup maraschino cherries, cut into fourths

In a large mixing bowl, beat sugar, shortening, egg, and vanilla until creamy. Sift flour, salt, baking soda, and baking powder together and add to creamed mixture. Stir in dates and nuts. Form into 1-inch balls and roll in crumbs. Place on a greased cookie sheet and put ¼ maraschino cherry on top of each. Bake at 350° F. for 10 minutes. Makes 3 to 4 dozen.

Whole Wheat Brownies

6 tablespoons cocoa
⅔ cup oil
4 eggs
2 cups sugar
1½ cups whole wheat flour
1 teaspoon baking powder
1 teaspoon salt
2 teaspoons vanilla
1 cup chopped nuts

In a large mixing bowl, beat together all ingredients except nuts. Fold in the nuts. Bake in a 9″ x 13″ x 2″ pan at 300° F. for about 40 minutes.

Topping variations

Frost with melted milk chocolate.
Spread with cream frosting flavored with mint. When set, spread with melted chocolate.
Cover with tiny marshmallows and sprinkle with chocolate chips. Return to hot oven for a few minutes to melt.
Roll gently in powdered sugar.

Peanut Butter Bars

¾ cup butter
¾ cup sugar
¾ cup brown sugar
2 eggs
¾ cup peanut butter
½ teaspoon salt
¾ teaspoon baking soda
½ teaspoon vanilla
1½ cups flour
1½ cups rolled oats
1 cup peanut butter
1 chocolate candy bar (8 ounces), melted

In a large mixing bowl, combine butter, sugars, eggs, ¾ cup peanut butter, salt, soda, and vanilla. Add flour and oats and blend well. Spread on a greased 10″ x 15″ cookie sheet and bake at 350° F. for 10 to 15 minutes or until light golden. Remove from oven and spread immediately with 1 cup peanut butter; when cool, spread with melted chocolate. Cut into squares.

Spicy Carrot Bars

1 cup water
1 cup raisins
1 cup sugar
⅓ cup shortening
1 large carrot, grated
1 teaspoon nutmeg
1 teaspoon cinnamon
1 teaspoon baking soda
¼ teaspoon salt
2 cups sifted flour
Chopped nuts, if desired

In a small saucepan cook water and raisins until raisins are soft. Set aside. Cream sugar and shortening together. Stir in grated carrot. Sift dry ingredients and add to creamed mixture along with raisin-water mixture and nuts. Spread into a greased 9″ x 13″ x 2″ pan and bake at 350° F. for 20 to 25 minutes. Cool, then frost with Buttermilk Icing.

Buttermilk Icing

1 cup sugar
½ cup butter
½ cup buttermilk
½ teaspoon baking soda
½ teaspoon vanilla

In a deep saucepan, combine sugar, butter, buttermilk, and baking soda; cook to softball stage. (Mixture boils over very easily, so watch it closely.) Cool 5 minutes. Add vanilla and beat until thick. Add chopped nuts, if desired.

Simply Scrumptious Squares

½ cup white corn syrup
½ cup brown sugar (packed)
½ cup peanut butter
1 cup Special K cereal
½ cup peanuts
½ cup thin pretzels
1 cup coconut
1 cup Corn Chex
1 cup Cheerios

Cook corn syrup and brown sugar together until mixture boils. Stir in remaining ingredients. Spread in an 8-inch square buttered pan. Cool 10 minutes and cut into squares.

Mincemeat Bars

2 packages (9 ounces each) dry mincemeat
1½ cups boiling water
¾ cup shortening
¾ cup sugar
⅓ cup molasses
1½ cups sifted flour
2 cups quick-cooking rolled oats
¾ teaspoon salt

Break the mincemeat into the boiling water. Cook, stirring constantly, 3 or 4 minutes. Set aside and let stand until cool. Cream shortening; add sugar gradually, beating until fluffy. Beat in molasses. Add flour, oats, and salt and mix well. Spread half the mixture in an ungreased 9" x 13" x 2" pan and press firmly with fingers. Spread the mincemeat filling over the oatmeal crust. Spread remaining oatmeal mixture evenly over filling. Bake at 350° F. for 30 minutes. Cut into bars.

Ellen's Things

½ cup butter
5 tablespoons cocoa
¼ cup sugar
1 teaspoon vanilla
1 egg
2 cups graham cracker crumbs
1 cup flaked coconut
½ cup finely chopped walnuts or pecans
2 cups powdered sugar
2 tablespoons Birds' custard powder (or use regular vanilla pudding powder)
½ cup butter
3 tablespoons milk
4 squares (1 ounce each) semisweet baking chocolate
1 tablespoon butter

Melt ½ cup butter in a heavy pan. Add cocoa, sugar, and vanilla, and stir until dissolved. Cool slightly, then beat in egg. Set aside. Mix the cracker crumbs, coconut, and nuts together and stir into the chocolate-butter mixture; press into an ungreased 9" x 13" x 2" pan. In a bowl beat the powdered sugar, custard powder, ½ cup butter, and milk until creamy. Spread over the chocolate mixture and chill until set. Melt the chocolate and 1 tablespoon butter in double boiler or microwave; cool just slightly and spread over the top. Cool, then cut into 48 1½-inch squares. These are very rich but delicious.

Romance Bars

1 cup flour
2 tablespoons sugar
½ cup butter
2 eggs
1¼ cups sugar
½ cup flaked coconut
1 cup chopped nuts
¼ cup cut-up maraschino cherries
2 tablespoons flour
½ teaspoon baking powder
1 teaspoon vanilla

Blend flour, sugar, and ½ cup butter well and press into an 8-inch or 9-inch square pan. Bake at 350° F. until lightly browned (about 25 minutes). Meanwhile prepare filling: Beat eggs. Add sugar and beat well. Stir in remaining ingredients and mix thoroughly. Pour over baked crust and return to oven for 20 minutes. Cool. Frost with favorite butter icing or melted chocolate bar. Cut into squares and serve. Makes 25 squares.

Baklava

1 pound shelled pecans, walnuts, or cashews
½ cup sugar
2 teaspoons allspice
1 teaspoon nutmeg
2 cups (1 pound) melted butter
1 pound phyllo leaves
2 cups sugar
1 cup water
4 to 5 tablespoons lemon juice

Chop the nuts fine and mix with ½ cup sugar, allspice, and nutmeg. In an 11" x 17" pan put one sheet of phyllo; spread with 1 tablespoon or a little more of melted butter. Repeat until you have 6 layers of buttered phyllo. Spread with ⅓ of the nut-spice mixture; then cover with 3 more layers of buttered phyllo. Repeat the nut mixture, then three more layers of phyllo. Add the last ⅓ of the nut mixture and cover with the rest of the phyllo leaves, buttering between each one and on the top layer. Be sure to keep the phyllo you are not using covered at all times with plastic wrap in order to keep it from drying out and becoming too brittle to handle. Cut the pastry layers into diamond shapes with a sharp knife. Bake at 300° F. for 1 hour.

About ½ hour before the baklava is done, combine in a saucepan 2 cups sugar and 1 cup water; cover and bring to a boil. Allow to boil for 1 minute, to wash down the crystals from the sides of the pan. Remove cover and boil until syrup spins a thread. Add lemon juice. Spoon hot syrup over the pastry as soon as it comes out of the oven. Let stand several hours or overnight before serving. Makes about 80 diamond-shaped pieces.

Cheesecake Bars

⅓ cup butter
½ cup brown sugar (packed)
1 cup sifted flour
½ cup chopped walnuts or pecans
1 package (8 ounces) cream cheese
½ cup sugar
1 egg
2 tablespoons milk
2 teaspoons lemon juice
½ teaspoon vanilla

Cream butter and brown sugar. Stir in flour and nuts. Reserve 1 cup of this mixture. Press remaining mixture into an 8-inch square pan, and bake at 350° F. about 12 or 13 minutes. Beat remaining ingredients together until smooth. Spread over crust, and sprinkle with reserved crumb mixture. Return to oven and bake 25 minutes more. Cool and cut into bars. Makes 25 bars.

PIES

Mother's Pumpkin Pie

¾ cup sugar
3 tablespoons cornstarch
1 teaspoon cinnamon
½ teaspoon each nutmeg, ginger, and salt
¼ teaspoon cloves
1¼ cups cooked, mashed pumpkin or winter squash
2 cups milk
2 large eggs, beaten
1 baked 9-inch pastry shell
1 cup cream, whipped and sweetened

Combine sugar, cornstarch, and spices in a heavy saucepan. Add squash and milk and blend thoroughly. Cook over medium heat, stirring constantly, until thick. Remove from heat and stir a small amount into eggs. Pour eggs back into pumpkin filling. Return to heat, and cook and stir for 3 to 4 minutes. Cool to room temperature. Pour into baked pie shell. Chill. Cover with whipped cream.

Pineapple/Peach Two-Crust Pie

Pastry for 9-inch two-crust pie
1 can (30 ounces) sliced peaches, or
   1 quart canned peaches, drained
1 can (16 ounces) crushed pineapple
   (do not drain)
2 tablespoons lemon juice
½ cup sugar
2 tablespoons instant tapioca
1 tablespoon melted butter

Line pie tin with pastry. Drain peaches and chop coarsely. Add pineapple with juice, lemon juice, sugar, and tapioca. Pour into pie shell and dribble melted butter over the top before covering with top pie crust. Bake at 450° F. for 10 minutes. Lower oven temperature to 375° F. and continue cooking for additional 40 minutes. Pie is delicious served with vanilla ice cream or whipped cream.

Pear Crunch Pie

1 unbaked 9-inch pie shell
1 cup flour
½ cup brown sugar, packed
½ cup butter
¼ teaspoon cinnamon
¼ teaspoon nutmeg
½ cup chopped nuts
1 can (30 ounces) pears, drained (reserve syrup)
¼ cup sugar
2 tablespoons cornstarch
⅛ teaspoon salt
¼ teaspoon nutmeg
1½ cups liquid (pear syrup plus water)
1 tablespoon butter
1 teaspoon grated lemon rind
1 tablespoon lemon juice

Prepare pie shell. Blend flour, brown sugar, ½ cup butter, cinnamon, and ¼ teaspoon nutmeg until they have the appearance of coarse crumbs; add chopped nuts and set aside for topping. Cut pear halves in half lengthwise and arrange in pie shell. Blend the sugar, cornstarch, salt, and ¼ teaspoon nutmeg and then stir in liquid. Cook, stirring, until thick. Add 1 tablespoon butter, lemon rind, and lemon juice and pour over pears. Sprinkle with topping. Bake at 425° F. for 10 minutes, then at 350° F. for 30 minutes or until lightly browned. Serve with a dollop of whipped cream on each piece.

Cinnamon Red Hot Apple Pie

Pastry for 10-inch two-crust pie
6 cups tart apples, peeled and sliced
¼ cup cinnamon red hots
¾ cup sugar
¼ cup instant tapioca (or flour)

Line a 10-inch pie tin with pastry. Mix all of the filling ingredients. Pour into pie shell; top with pastry. Bake at 400° F. for 10 minutes. Reduce heat to 350° F.; bake for 35 minutes more. Remove from oven, brush with butter, and sprinkle with granulated sugar. Return to oven for a few minutes.

Double Apple Pie

Pastry for 9-inch two-crust pie
4 cups peeled and sliced cooking apples
1 can (6 ounces) frozen apple juice concentrate
3 tablespoons instant tapioca
1 teaspoon cinnamon

Line a 9-inch pie plate with pastry. Combine remaining ingredients and pour into pie shell. Cover with pastry. Bake at 400° F. for 10 minutes. Reduce heat to 350° F. and continue baking for 25 minutes.

Give every man thine ear, but few thy voice; take each man's censure, but reserve thy judgment. (William Shakespeare)

French Cherry Pie

1 can sweetened condensed milk
⅓ cup lemon juice
1 teaspoon vanilla
½ teaspoon almond extract
½ cup whipping cream, whipped
1 baked 9-inch pie shell*

Combine condensed milk, lemon juice, vanilla, and almond extract in a saucepan. Cook over medium heat, stirring constantly, until mixture thickens. Fold in whipped cream and spoon into pie shell. Place in refrigerator while you make cherry topping.

Cherry Topping

1 can (1 pound) pitted sour cherries, drained (reserve juice)
¼ cup sugar
⅔ cup juice from cherries
1 tablespoon cornstarch
2 or 3 drops red food coloring

Combine sugar, juice, cornstarch, and coloring and cook over medium heat, stirring constantly, until mixture thickens. Add cherries; stir and cook for 5 minutes more. Cool. Spread over cream filling. Return to refrigerator and chill. Top with whipped cream, if desired.

*Add chopped almonds to pie crust for extra flavor. A graham cracker crust is also good.

Mincemeat Cream Cheese Pie

1 baked 9-inch pastry shell
2 scant cups mincemeat
12 ounces cream cheese
2 eggs
½ cup sugar
1 tablespoon lemon juice
1 teaspoon grated lemon rind
1 cup sour cream
2 tablespoons sugar
1 teaspoon vanilla

Place mincemeat in pie shell. Cream together the cream cheese, eggs, ½ cup sugar, lemon juice, and rind, and pour over mincemeat. Bake at 375° F. for 20 minutes. Remove from oven. Combine sour cream, 2 tablespoons sugar, and vanilla; pour over hot pie, and bake 10 minutes more. Refrigerate at least 5 hours before serving. Pie is very rich, so cut in small pieces. Serves 8 to 12.

Banana Split Pie

1 graham cracker crust
2 bananas
1½ pints ice cream (any flavor)
½ cup chocolate ice cream topping
½ cup strawberry jam or topping
1 cup heavy cream
2 tablespoons sugar
1 teaspoon vanilla

Prepare graham cracker crust, using favorite recipe. Slice one banana in the bottom of the crust. Cover with ⅓ of the slightly softened ice cream. Cover with chocolate topping. Layer on the second third of the ice cream. Cover with second banana, sliced. Top with strawberry jam. Layer on the third portion of ice cream. Whip cream and flavor with sugar and vanilla. Decorate the top of the pie with the whipped cream and, if desired, bits of cherries and chocolate. Freeze until serving time. If you prefer the whipped cream soft, put it on just before serving. Serves 8.

Walnut Pie

1 unbaked 9-inch pie shell
3 eggs
⅔ cup sugar
½ teaspoon salt
⅓ cup butter, melted
1 cup dark corn syrup
½ teaspoon cinnamon
½ teaspoon nutmeg
½ teaspoon cloves
1 cup chopped walnuts
Whipped cream, sweetened to taste

Prepare pie shell, using favorite recipe. Mix remaining ingredients except walnuts and beat well. Add walnuts. Pour into pie shell. Bake at 375° F. for 40 to 50 minutes. Serve with whipped cream. *Note:* Flavor improves the second day.

You can accomplish much if you don't care who gets the credit. (Ronald Reagan)

Frosty Fry Pie

1 cup flour
½ cup butter
½ cup brown sugar
¼ cup chopped pecans
3 cups skim milk or reconstituted powdered milk
½ cup lemon juice
½ cup evaporated milk
1½ cups granulated sugar

Over medium heat, cook the flour, butter, brown sugar, and pecans in a heavy skillet until golden brown, stirring constantly. Reserve ½ cup of mixture. Press remaining crumbs into a 9-inch pie tin. Combine the skim milk, lemon juice, evaporated milk, and sugar; mix well and freeze. Whip frozen mixture in a blender and pour into the crumb shell. Sprinkle reserved crumbs on top to form a wreath around the edge. Decorate center with maraschino cherries and mint leaves. Freeze. Serves 8.

Variation

Add two or three mint leaves when you blend the frozen mixture.

Butterscotch Tarts

2 tablespoons butter
1 cup brown sugar, packed
½ teaspoon vanilla
1 egg, beaten

Mix all ingredients thoroughly and put 1 tablespoon in each unbaked tart shell in muffin tin. Bake at 375° F. to 400° F. for 10 to 15 minutes or until golden brown. Makes 12 to 16 large tarts or 3 dozen tea-size tarts.

Tart Pastry or Sweet Paste

2 cups cake flour
½ cup butter or margarine, softened
⅓ cup powdered sugar
½ teaspoon salt
2 tablespoons cold water

Put all ingredients together in mixing bowl and mix on low speed until mixture forms a dough. Roll and cut in circles to fit tart pans or muffin tins.

Variation

Add 1 cup pecans or press whole pecans into each tart before baking.

As if you could kill time without injuring eternity. (Henry David Thoreau)

Practically Perfect Pie

½ cup butter
1 cup sugar
2 egg yolks
2 squares (1 ounce each) unsweetened baking chocolate, melted and cooled
1 teaspoon vanilla
½ cup sifted flour
2 egg whites, beaten into soft peaks
½ cup chopped pecans
1 quart vanilla, orange ripple, or other favorite flavor ice cream

Cream together butter and sugar until light and fluffy. Add egg yolks one at a time, beating well after each addition. Blend in chocolate and vanilla; gradually add flour. Fold beaten egg whites into batter along with pecans. Spread evenly in a 9-inch pie plate; bake at 325° F. for 30 to 35 minutes. Cool. Just before serving, spoon ice cream over pie.

Chocolate Angel Strata

2 egg whites
½ teaspoon vinegar
¼ teaspoon salt
½ cup sugar
1 baked 9-inch pie shell

Beat egg whites, vinegar, and salt until stiff. Gradually add sugar, beating to stiff peaks. Spread meringue in pie shell and bake at 325° F. for 15 to 18 minutes, until lightly browned. Cool.

Chocolate Filling

1 cup (6-ounce package) chocolate chips
2 egg yolks
¼ cup water
1 cup whipping cream
1 tablespoon sugar
Slivered almonds

Melt chocolate chips in top of double boiler, over boiling water. Beat egg yolks with water; add to chocolate and beat over hot water for ½ minute. Spread 3 heaping tablespoons of chocolate mixture over cooled meringue. Chill remainder of filling. Whip cream and add sugar. Spread half of this mixture over pie. Fold in chilled chocolate and remaining whipped cream and spread over pie. Top with a few sprinkles of slivered almonds. Chill at least 4 hours.

Rest is not quitting the busy career;
Rest is the fitting of self to one's sphere;
It's loving and serving the highest and best;
It's onward, unswerving; and this is true rest.
—Goethe

DESSERTS

Never-fail Meringue Shells

4 egg whites (room temperature)
1 cup sugar
1 teaspoon vanilla
1 teaspoon white vinegar

Beat egg whites until stiff and dry. While still beating, slowly add sugar, then vanilla and vinegar. Continue beating until extremely stiff. On the underside of an ungreased cookie sheet drop mixture in 6 large portions. Allow 2 inches around for expansion. With a spoon, depress a well in the center of each. (Meringue may also be formed with a large pastry bag and rosette tip.) Bake on middle shelf of oven at 250° F. for 1 hour or until pinkish-beige in color. Test by touching. If sticky, return to oven for a little longer. With spatula, scoop carefully from baking sheet immediately onto wax paper or dessert dishes; if meringues cool before being removed from pan, they will break. Fill with fresh fruit or ice cream with sauce and top with whipped cream.

Elegant Creamy Cheesecake

9-inch graham cracker crust
2 packages (8 ounces each) cream cheese
½ cup sugar
2 eggs
1 teaspoon vanilla
1½ cups sour cream
¼ cup sugar
1 teaspoon vanilla

With a blender or mixer beat together the cream cheese, ½ cup sugar, eggs, and 1 teaspoon vanilla until well blended and creamy. Pour into graham cracker crust and bake at 350° F. for 30 minutes. While this bakes, stir the sour cream, ¼ cup sugar, and 1 teaspoon vanilla together. Spread over the hot cheesecake and return to oven for 5 minutes more. Serve plain or with favorite fruit topping, such as raspberry, blueberry, or strawberry. Serves 8 to 10.

Easy Cheesecake

¼ cup butter, melted
1½ cups dry bread crumbs or Puffed Wheat cereal, lightly crushed
1 package (8 ounces) cream cheese or cottage cheese, or ½ cup of each
½ cup frozen apple juice concentrate
½ cup cream or half-and-half
3 eggs
1 teaspoon vanilla, lemon, or almond flavoring

Mix melted butter with crumbs and press into a 9-inch square pan. Set aside. Put cream cheese, apple juice, and cream into a blender and blend until smooth. Add eggs one at a time, beating between each addition. Add flavoring and pour into crust. Bake at 350° F. for 25 minutes. Turn heat off and leave in oven for 2 hours—do not open the oven door until time is up. Remove from oven, and top with crushed or sliced fruit. Makes 8 to 10 servings.

Grandma's Apple Brown Betty

2 cups fine bread crumbs
¼ cup brown sugar
2 tablespoons butter, melted
6 to 8 cooking apples
2 tablespoons lemon juice
¾ cup brown sugar
Dash of salt
1 teaspoon cinnamon (or to taste)

Combine crumbs, brown sugar, and butter. Set aside. Peel, core, and slice apples. Stir in lemon juice, brown sugar, salt, and cinnamon; coat apples thoroughly. Put half the apples in a buttered baking dish. Cover with half the crumb mixture. Add remaining apples and top with remaining crumbs. Bake uncovered at 325° F. for about 1 hour or until apple slices are fork tender. Serve hot with a scoop of vanilla ice cream on each serving. Serves 8.

Trifle ✓

1 frozen pound cake (12 ounces) or
  Butter Sponge Cake (p. 78) or
  "A Cup of Each" Sponge Cake (p. 79)
½ cup jam (any flavor)
¾ cup orange juice
1 teaspoon rum flavoring
4 cups strawberries, washed, hulled, and sliced
  (or other fruit in season), or 1 can (30 ounces)
  pears, peaches, or apricots, cut up and
  well drained
1 small package (3¾ ounces) regular vanilla
  pudding (not instant)
3 cups milk
1 cup whipping cream, whipped and sweetened

Cut cake into 16 thin slices. Spread 8 slices with jam and top with remaining 8 slices. Cut each sandwich into 3 lady-finger-size pieces and arrange on bottom and standing up around sides of a large glass bowl. Combine orange juice and rum flavoring, and sprinkle on cake. Let soak in refrigerator for a few minutes. Place on cake the 4 cups of fruit. Cook pudding, using the 3 cups milk; cool. Pour over the cake and fruit and chill overnight. When ready to serve, spread on the sweetened whipped cream. This delectable dessert came from England, where the provident woman was looking for a way to use leftovers. She put into a bowl "a trifle of this and a trifle of that." There are almost as many variations as there are cooks. It is a good way to use up leftover cake.

Variation

Spoon a layer of partially set red gelatin over the cake layer.

Favorite Make-ahead Dessert ✓

1 frozen pound cake
1 large package (12 ounces) chocolate chips
1 cup sour cream

The day before serving, slice off rounded brown top of cake, leaving a flat surface. Slice cake lengthwise, forming 5 or 6 thin layers, and arrange in order on waxed paper. Melt chocolate chips and sour cream in top of double boiler over boiling water. Place bottom layer of cake on serving platter and ice with chocolate mixture. Repeat layering. Frost on top and sides with chocolate mixture. Place in freezer until ready to serve. Garnish with fresh mint leaves and shaved chocolate; slice and serve. Serves 6.

Apple Crisp Pudding

1 cup graham cracker crumbs
1 tablespoon flour
1 cup chopped nuts
1¼ cups firmly packed brown sugar
1 tablespoon grated orange rind
Dash of salt
½ teaspoon nutmeg
½ teaspoon cinnamon
½ cup melted butter or margarine
2 tablespoons lemon juice
4 or 5 tart apples

Mix together all ingredients except the apples. Peel, core, and thinly slice the apples. Place half the apples in a 9-inch square buttered baking dish. Sprinkle with ⅓ of the crumb mixture. Add the remaining apples; cover with the remaining crumb mixture. Bake at 350° F. for 45 minutes. Serve warm with cream or ice cream. Serves 8.

Frosty Lemon Dessert

1½ cups biscuit mix
2 tablespoons sugar
3 tablespoons butter
3 eggs, separated
1 tablespoon sugar
1 teaspoon grated lemon peel
2 tablespoons lemon juice
½ cup sugar
1 cup whipping cream

Mix the biscuit mix, 2 tablespoons sugar, and butter until crumbly. Reserve ½ cup of mixture. Press remaining mixture into a 9-inch square pan and bake at 375° F. until light brown, about 12 minutes. Spread reserved crumbs on a cookie sheet and bake until light brown, about 6 minutes. Combine the egg yolks, 1 tablespoon sugar, lemon peel, and lemon juice and cook over low heat until thick, stirring constantly. Cool. Beat the egg whites until foamy; add ½ cup sugar, 1 tablespoon at a time, and continue beating until stiff and glossy. Do not underbeat. Whip cream thoroughly. Carefully fold egg white and whipped cream into lemon mixture. Spread over crust in pan and sprinkle with baked crumb mixture. Freeze until firm, at least 4 hours. Let sit at room temperature just a few minutes; then cut and serve. Serves 8 to 10.

Quick Peach Crisp

1 can (30 ounces) or 1 quart peaches, drained and sliced
¼ teaspoon nutmeg
¼ teaspoon cinnamon
⅓ cup flour
1 cup oatmeal
½ cup brown sugar (packed)
⅓ cup melted butter

Place drained peaches in an 8-inch square baking dish and sprinkle with nutmeg and cinnamon. Combine the rest of ingredients and spoon over peaches. Bake at 350° F. for 35 minutes. Serve hot either plain, or with cream or milk poured over, or topped with a spoonful of vanilla ice cream. Serves 6 to 8. This can be made in a minute and baked while you are getting dinner on the table.

Espuma de Chocolate

3 ounces milk chocolate
2 tablespoons instant Pero
4 egg yolks
4 egg whites
¼ cup sugar
1½ cups whipping cream

In a double boiler over boiling water, heat chocolate and Pero until chocolate is melted. Remove from heat and cool. Beat yolks until light. Add sugar and continue beating until fluffy. Add cooled chocolate and mix well. Beat whites

until stiff but not dry. Fold into chocolate mixture slowly and carefully. Whip cream and fold into mixture. Pour into custard cups or demitasse cups. Chill at least 6 hours. To make this dessert extra fancy, pour a little melted sweet chocolate in the bottom of each custard cup. Before serving, dip briefly in hot water and unmold on serving dishes. Garnish with whipped cream and cherry. Serves 8.

Pero Bavarian

1 cup fine graham cracker crumbs
¼ cup melted butter
1 envelope unflavored gelatin
½ cup cold water
½ cup sugar
1 tablespoon instant Pero
¼ teaspoon salt
1⅔ cups evaporated milk

Combine crumbs and butter. Press on bottom of an 8-inch square pan. Chill until needed. Stir gelatin into cold water. Let stand 5 minutes until dissolved. Add sugar, Pero, salt, and 1 cup of the evaporated milk. Chill in small bowl of electric mixer until firm. Beat with electric mixer at low speed until mixture is broken up. Beat in remaining ⅔ cup evaporated milk. Beat at high speed until mixture fills bowl. Pour over crumbs in baking dish. Sprinkle with chocolate decorettes or shaved chocolate. Chill until firm (about 2 hours) or freeze. Serves 9.

Gizmos

3 squares (1 ounce each) semisweet chocolate
2 tablespoons butter
2 tablespoons rum flavoring
1 egg white
1 tablespoon instant Pero
1 cup heavy cream
4 tablespoons sugar
½ cup fine macaroon crumbs
½ cup toasted almonds, finely chopped

Melt chocolate and butter in top of double boiler over boiling water. Add rum flavoring and set aside to cool. Beat egg white until stiff; fold in

Pero. Whip cream until stiff; add sugar. Into whipped cream fold the Pero and chocolate mixtures. Add crumbs and almonds. Pour into 2-ounce paper cupcake cups and freeze overnight or for several days. Just before serving, remove from freezer and peel off the paper cups. If desired, top with whipped cream and slivered almonds. Makes 6 to 8 servings.

Custard Rice Pudding

4 eggs
3 cups milk
¾ cup brown sugar
½ teaspoon salt
1½ teaspoons vanilla
¼ cup white raisins (optional)
1 cup cooked rice
Nutmeg

Beat the eggs until frothy. Add milk, brown sugar, salt, and vanilla, and blend thoroughly. Stir in raisins and rice. Pour into buttered 2-quart casserole dish and bake at 325° F. for approximately 25 minutes or until pudding starts to thicken. Stir thoroughly. Sprinkle top with nutmeg. Continue baking until custard on top is set. Serve warm with a dollop of sweetened whipped cream or sour cream. Serves 6 to 8.

Strawberry Orange Ice

1¾ cups orange juice
½ cup lemon juice
1¾ cups sugar
⅛ teaspoon salt
3 pints strawberries, washed and hulled

Stir juices, sugar, and salt together. Place ⅓ of mixture and ⅓ of berries in a blender and blend until combined but not smooth. Pour into pan. Repeat twice. Cover and freeze until frozen one inch around edge. Put in a mixing bowl and beat until smooth. Return to pan and freeze until firm, at least 4 hours or overnight. Let sit on counter about 10 minutes before serving, or let sit in refrigerator while eating dinner. Makes 20 servings.

Three-of-a-Kind Ice Cream

3 oranges
3 lemons
3 bananas
3 cups milk
3 cups whipping cream
1½ cups sugar

Squeeze oranges and lemons. Add mashed bananas to juice and chill. Mix together milk, cream, and sugar. Add banana mixture to milk mixture. Freeze in ice-cream freezer according to manufacturer's instructions. Makes 2 quarts. *Note:* Ice cream may be kept in freezer for later use; whip before serving.

Fruity Ice Cream

3 cups crushed fruit
1 can (12 ounces) apple juice concentrate
2 egg yolks
1 pint whipping cream

Mix together fruit and half of the apple juice. Heat other half of apple juice and add lightly beaten egg yolks, stirring. Continue cooking until mixture thickens. Cool; add to fruit mixture. Whip cream until it holds its shape; fold into fruit mixture. Pile into a metal bread pan or three 1-pint containers. Freeze in freezer compartment of refrigerator. Serves 6 to 8. *Note:* Ice cream will have texture of a mousse. It may also be made in an ice-cream freezer and stored in freezer.

Fruit Freeze

1 quart frozen fruit purée (apricot, peach, cherry, plum, or grape)
1 can (6 ounces) frozen orange or apple juice concentrate
1 cup cream or yogurt

Partially thaw fruit purée so it can be cut into chunks. Put in blender with other ingredients and blend until smooth. Serve at once, or if it isn't stiff enough, return to freezer until ready. Serves 8. *Note:* This is a good dessert for those who can't eat refined sugar.

Strawberry Angel Freeze

1 cup flour
½ cup butter
¼ cup brown sugar
1 package (4 ounces) sliced almonds
2 packages (10 ounces each) frozen strawberries
2 egg whites
1 cup sugar
1 teaspoon vanilla
½ pint whipping cream

Mix together flour, butter, brown sugar, and almonds. Spread on a cookie sheet and bake at 350° F. until light golden brown, stirring occasionally. Cool. Spread half of crumb mixture in bottom of a 9″ x 13″ x 2″ pan. In a mixing bowl combine strawberries, egg whites, sugar, and vanilla; whip at high speed for twenty minutes. Whip cream. Fold the whipped cream into the strawberry mixture. Pour over the crumb mixture. Top with remaining crumbs and freeze. To serve, cut into squares. Serves 12 to 15.

Favorite Fruit Ice Cream

4 packages (10 ounces each) frozen raspberries or strawberries, thawed, or 4½ cups of any fresh fruit
4 cups sugar
2 quarts half-and-half
1 pint sour cream
Juice of 3 lemons
Milk

In a blender combine until creamy 1 package of the fruit, 1 cup sugar, 1 cup half-and-half, and ½ cup sour cream. Pour into a 6-quart ice-cream freezer can. Repeat 3 more times. Add the rest of the half-and-half, lemon juice, and enough milk to fill can to within 4 inches of the top. Stir well. Freeze according to manufacturer's instructions. If made day before, allow to soften slightly at room temperature before serving. Makes 6 quarts.

---

*There is no verbal vitamin more potent than praise.
(Frederick B. Harris)*

Yogurt Popsicles

1 quart plain yogurt
⅔ cup powdered milk
⅔ cup water
1 teaspoon vanilla
1 can (12 ounces) frozen orange juice concentrate

Combine all ingredients and mix in blender until smooth. Pour into 2-ounce paper cups. Put a stick in the center of each and freeze. Makes 2 dozen popsicles.

Chocolate Sauce

1 tall can evaporated milk
3 cups sugar
3 squares unsweetened baking chocolate
1 teaspoon vanilla

Combine milk, sugar, and chocolate in a heavy saucepan. Heat over low heat, stirring constantly, until the sugar is entirely dissolved, about 15 minutes. Do not boil. Pour into blender and beat at high speed until mixture thickens. Add vanilla. Makes approximately 1 quart. Use as a topping for ice cream or cake, or stir 1 tablespoon into 1 cup of hot milk for delicious hot chocolate.

Quick and Easy Syrups

Peach Syrup

In blender combine 2 cups canned peaches, drained, with ½ cup melted butter and ½ cup honey. Store in refrigerator, and heat before serving.

Orange Syrup

In a saucepan bring to a boil 1 small can (6 ounces) frozen orange juice concentrate. Remove from heat. Add 1 cup sugar and ½ cup butter, and stir until dissolved.

Coconut Syrup

Combine 2 cups maple syrup and 1 cup grated coconut; blend well in blender.

Fruit Syrup

Add ⅓ cup water to 2 cups of any flavor jam or jelly; blend well and bring to boil. Serve hot or cold.

Fresh Peach-Pineapple Topping

Place equal parts of sliced peaches and pineapple chunks in freezer containers. Cover with pineapple juice. Freeze. Thaw to slush stage and serve over ice cream or Belgian waffles.

Divine Chocolate Pecan Ice Cream Topping

1 pound milk chocolate
¼ cup cooking oil
2 cups pecans

Melt the chocolate with the oil in a double boiler over hot water, stirring constantly. Add pecans. Serve hot over ice cream, or store in refrigerator in a tightly covered container. To serve, place container in a pan of hot water until chocolate melts.

Caramel Sauce

1½ cups brown sugar (packed)
⅔ cup evaporated milk
⅔ cup light corn syrup
¼ cup butter or margarine

Stir all ingredients together in a heavy saucepan; bring to a boil over medium heat and cook 3 minutes, stirring constantly. If the sauce separates slightly while cooking, blend in blender 1 minute. May be thinned, if desired, with additional corn syrup or cream. Serve hot or cold over ice cream. Makes 3 cups.

We have no more right to consume happiness without producing it than to consume wealth without producing it. (George Bernard Shaw)

Homemade Sweetened Condensed Milk

1 cup hot water
2 cups sugar
¼ cup butter
4 cups instant dry milk powder

Blend hot water and sugar in a saucepan and stir over medium heat until sugar is dissolved. Place in blender and gradually add dry milk until blended smooth. This makes the equivalent of 2 cans (15 ounces each) of sweetened condensed milk.

Dulce de Leche

Carmelize Homemade Sweetened Condensed Milk by placing in a canning jar with a tight lid. Leave at least 1 inch at top for expansion. Put jar on a rack in a pan of boiling water; cover and boil for at least 3 hours. Use as a topping on ice cream or spread on cookies or cake.

Bitter-Sweet Chocolate Candy

2 squares unsweetened baking chocolate
1 rounded tablespoon frozen apple juice concentrate
1 teaspoon butter

Heat all together over hot water or very low heat, stirring until blended and smooth. Add nuts or raisins, if desired. Drop by spoonfuls onto wax paper and set in the refrigerator to harden. For sweeter candy, use more apple juice concentrate and heat a bit longer. *Note:* This is a special treat for those who can't eat refined sugar.

The soul that perpetually overflows with kindness and sympathy will always be cheerful. (Parke Goodwin)

The second mile

Second-Mile Treats

Fruit Cup Treat	98	Five-minute Granola	99
Fruit Cake	98	Gift Salami	99
Caramel Corn	98	Jerky	99
Honey Corn	98	Popped Wheat	100
Granola	99	Snack or Trail Mix	100

SECOND-MILE TREATS

Compassionate service is always a worthwhile Sunday activity, especially if the service is accompanied by a gift of food. Homemade treats tell the recipient that you really care, that you have taken the time to prepare something special just for him or her. Whether it's the new mother just home with her tiny baby, a lonely widow or widower, a family mourning the loss of a loved one, someone who has just received a special honor, or just someone to whom you want to say "I care," your gift will help lift a heart or lighten a load.

In this section are a few of our favorite second-mile treats that we have prepared for special friends and neighbors. But don't feel restricted to just these few ideas. Throughout this book you'll find many recipes for food gifts: homemade loaves of bread; cakes, cookies, pies, and other special desserts; soups and chowders; dips for chips and vegetables; casseroles; salads and fresh vegetables from your garden.

Add a colorful bow or cover a jar lid with a bonnet of gingham. To add even more fun to your gift giving, here are some additional ideas:

1. Give a jar of special jam and attach this message: "If you're ever in a jam, call ———" (add your name and phone number).

2. Give a jar of relish with this message: "We relish your friendship."

3. Give a small pot of real or artificial flowers with this message: "Bloom where you are planted."

4. Attach to a plastic or wooden mixing spoon: "May your heart be stirred as you fulfill your role."

5. Arrange some daisies in a small vase and attach a card that reads: "We must adjust to routine in our lives. Remember, God hasn't grown tired of growing daisies yet."

6. Give a favorite candy bar to which you have attached a special message. For example:

Mounds: "Mounds of blessings await you."

Powerhouse: "For a house of knowledge, read the scriptures daily."

Rocky Road: "If you travel a rocky road, remember that you are not alone."

Rally: "Rally 'round."

Almond Joy: "Joy means giving of yourself."

U-No: "U-No what? We appreciate you!"

Charm candies: "——— (add name of recipient) charms me!"

7. Print a message on a small card, glue the card onto a popsicle stick, and place the stick in a pot containing a plant. Here are some possible messages:

"Cultivate your mind so it will be fertile enough to accept the word of the Lord."

"Plant seeds of faith, hope, and charity deep within your soul."

"Weed your life of undesirable traits that might harm the growth of your testimony."

"Don't be afraid of the plow, because nothing grows without some pain and sorrow."

"Keep your garden moist with a few tears and much love."

"Watch for the blossoms and reap the rich harvest of your testimony."

8. Give a box of crayons with this little poem:

It's Up to Me

Outside my window dawns a day
That could be bright or could be gray.
It could be filled with tasks well done,
With love and friends, with joy and fun.
The gift of choice is mine to use,
To COLOR well, in brightest hues.

Fruit Cup Treat

4 grapefruit
4 oranges
4 bananas
1 can (20 ounces) pineapple chunks with juice
9 maraschino cherries, cut up
2 or 3 tablespoons sugar (or to taste)
1 teaspoon grenadine syrup
Juice of 1 lime

Into a large bowl, peel and cut up the grapefruit, oranges, and bananas. Add remaining ingredients and chill. Add orange juice if more liquid is desired. Spoon into pint or quart jars, decorated with ribbon or square of gingham. This is delicious as a breakfast cup or dessert, or as a topping for ice cream.

Fruit Cake

1 cup dried apple slices
2 cups dried apricots
1 cup golden raisins
2 cups dates
2 cups other dried fruit, such as peaches, pears, cherries, figs
1 can (12 ounces) frozen orange juice concentrate
2 cups walnuts
2 cups pecans
2 cups almonds
3½ cups flour
3½ teaspoons baking powder
1 teaspoon salt
1 teaspoon cinnamon
1 teaspoon cloves
1 teaspoon allspice
8 eggs, well beaten
½ cup water
2 cups honey
1 teaspoon vanilla
¼ cup light corn syrup
1 tablespoon water

In a large bowl, combine the dried fruits; pour the orange juice concentrate over all and stir in. If fruit is extremely dry, you may need a bit more juice. Allow to stand 1 hour. Stir in the nuts. Measure and sift together the dry ingredients and combine with fruit and nut mixture; stir until well coated. Combine the well-beaten eggs, water, honey, and vanilla. Pour over fruit and nut mixture and mix well. Press into a large 11" x 17" x 2" baking pan. Decorate top with rows of nuts and date halves. Bake at 300° F. about 2 hours. Just before removing from oven, combine corn syrup and water and bring to a boil. While cake is still hot, brush top with glaze. Cool completely and cut into 10 individual cakes each about 2½" x 8". Wrap in plastic wrap and decorate with ribbon.

Caramel Corn

4 quarts popcorn
½ pound butter
1 heaping cup sugar
2 cups nuts—any kind or combination

Take unpopped kernels out of popped corn. Mix the popped corn and nuts in a large bowl or pan. Melt the butter and sugar together over high heat in a heavy pan, stirring constantly with a flat-edged wooden spoon. The syrup will go through three stages: (1) It looks like mixture of butter and sugar. (2) Then it looks like melted cheese and falls off the spoon in clumps. (3) The color changes to caramel and the syrup thins and pours smoothly off the spoon. If the butter and sugar should separate as it goes into stage 3, watch the color. When the color is light golden, remove from heat and stir until butter is blended back in. Pour syrup over corn, stirring to coat everything with a thin coating. Pour out on a tray to cool. Break apart into small pieces.

Honey Corn

6 cups popped corn
1 cup peanuts, cashews, pecans, sesame seeds, or sunflower seeds
½ cup honey
¼ cup butter, melted

Mix together all ingredients and spread on a cookie sheet. Bake at 350° F. for 10 minutes.

Granola

8 cups rolled oats (not instant)
6 cups rolled wheat
2 cups wheat germ
4 cups coconut
½ cup sesame seeds
2 cups chopped nuts
2 cups brown sugar
1 cup oil
1 cup water
¾ cup honey
1 tablespoon vanilla
2 teaspoons salt

Combine oats, wheat, wheat germ, coconut, seeds, and nuts in a large bowl. Combine remaining ingredients in a saucepan and bring to a boil. Remove from heat and pour over mixture in bowl. Stir to coat evenly. Spread on two large cookie sheets and bake at 300° F. until lightly browned (about 20 minutes), stirring occasionally.

Five-minute Granola

2½ cups rolled oats*
2½ cups rolled wheat*
½ cup oil
½ cup honey
2 cups coconut
2 cups almonds or other nuts or seeds
2 cups fresh-ground whole wheat flour
5 cups rolled grains*
2 cups raisins or dates
Cinnamon, if desired

In a large baking pan combine the oats and wheat, oil, honey, coconut, almonds, and flour. Bake at 425° F. for about 5 minutes, stirring once. Remove from heat and stir in the 5 cups of grains and the raisins or dates. Sprinkle with cinnamon and stir in. Cool thoroughly. Store in airtight containers.

*Any combination of grains may be used, including triticale and rye, in addition to or in place of oats and wheat. Do not use instant or quick-cooking varieties, however.

Gift Salami

4 pounds ground beef (maximum fat content)
¼ cup curing salt*
2 tablespoons liquid smoke
1½ teaspoons garlic powder
1½ teaspoons ground pepper (or whole peppercorns)

Mix all together in a large bowl; cover and chill 24 hours. Divide mixture into 4 portions. Shape each portion into a log in an 8-inch piece of nylon net. Roll tightly; tie ends with string. Place salami logs on a rack in a broiler pan and bake at 225° F. for 4 hours. Remove from oven and cut away the net. Pat rolls with paper towels to absorb excess fat. Cool slightly, then wrap in foil and refrigerate or freeze. Makes about 3 pounds.

*Curing salt may be purchased at a food locker plant.

Jerky

1 teaspoon salt
1 teaspoon liquid smoke
⅓ teaspoon garlic powder
⅓ teaspoon grated black pepper
⅓ teaspoon monosodium glutamate (optional)
1 teaspoon onion powder
¼ cup soy sauce
¼ cup Worcestershire sauce
1½ pounds lean beef, venison, or turkey, thinly sliced

Combine all ingredients except the meat. Toss meat in mixture. Arrange the meat slices on a large, flat pan. Place in oven preheated to 200° F.; cook for 8 to 12 hours, turning several times for even drying. Or hang the meat outside on a string to dry in a cool, airy place. Store in plastic bags in refrigerator or freezer. Makes ¾ pound dried meat.

Do not pray for tasks equal to your powers. Pray for powers equal to your tasks. Then the doing of your work will be no miracle, but you shall be the miracle.

Popped Wheat

2 cups wheat
1 cup cooking oil
Garlic salt to taste

Soak wheat overnight; drain well. Dry on paper towel. Heat oil about ¼-inch deep in heavy skillet. Cook wheat until browned and light. Drain well and season with garlic salt to taste. Serves 4 to 6.

He who chooses the beginning of a road chooses the place to which it leads.

Snack or Trail Mix

Large shredded unsweetened coconut
Banana chips
Pecans or other favorite nuts
Chopped sugared dates
Golden raisins
Dried fruits, cut up

In a large bowl, combine ingredients in proportions you desire. Store in airtight containers. Snack mixture may be put in small plastic bags when you're packing lunches, or tucked in a pocket for skiing, running, or hiking. It also makes a nutritious—and delicious—after-school treat.

Feeding the multitudes

Feeding the Multitudes

FEEDING THE MULTITUDES

For the occasional Sabbath when you have a large family gathering or evening fireside, we have included a few large-quantity recipes that can all be prepared ahead. In other sections you'll find other recipes for large groups, including salads, desserts, and beverages, to round out your menu.

Meatball Chowder

> 2 pounds ground beef
> 2 teaspoons seasoned salt
> Pepper to taste
> 2 eggs, beaten
> ¼ cup chopped parsley
> ⅓ cup fine cracker crumbs
> 2 tablespoons milk
> 4 to 6 onions, cut in eighths
> 2 bay leaves
> 6 cups water
> 6 cups tomato juice
> 6 beef bouillon cubes
> 3 cups sliced carrots
> 3 cups chopped celery
> 3 potatoes, diced
> ¼ cup raw long-grain rice
> 1 tablespoon sugar
> 2 teaspoons salt
> 1 tablespoon butter
> 1 can (12 ounces) Mexicorn

Mix together ground beef, seasoned salt, pepper, eggs, parsley, crumbs, and milk. Form into meatballs (about 40), each about the size of a walnut. Dip lightly in flour and brown in oil. Drain thoroughly. In a large kettle (about 3 gallons) combine all the rest of the ingredients except the corn. Bring to a boil and simmer gently until vegetables are almost tender (about 15 minutes). Add meatballs and simmer 15 minutes more. Add corn and serve. Makes 7 quarts of chowder.

Company Cheese Soup

> 3 carrots, diced
> 1 small onion, chopped
> 6 large ribs celery, chopped
> 1 jar (16 ounces) Cheez Whiz
> 6 quarts water
> 10 tablespoons chicken-flavored soup base or 20 chicken bouillon cubes
> 1½ cups butter, melted
> 1½ cups flour
> Salt and pepper to taste
> 1 package (10 ounces) frozen peas

Boil carrots, onion, and celery together in a small amount of water until tender. Remove lid from Cheez Whiz, and warm cheese in the jar in 2 inches of water until melted. Heat to boiling the 6 quarts water and the chicken base. Blend butter and flour together and stir vigorously into soup. Add seasonings to taste. Add drained vegetables and frozen peas and simmer 5 to 10 minutes. Add cheese. Serve. Makes 8 quarts.

Spaghetti for a Crowd

> 1 pound mushrooms
> 2 tablespoons butter
> 3 pounds lean ground beef
> 2 tablespoons salt
> 2 teaspoons chili powder
> 1 teaspoon rosemary
> ¼ teaspoon marjoram
> 2 bay leaves
> 4 cloves garlic, peeled and cut fine
> 6 cans (6 ounces each) tomato paste
> 6 cans water
> 2 cans (8 ounces each) tomato sauce
> 1 cup grated Monterey Jack cheese
> 2 pounds spaghetti

Sauté mushrooms in butter until tender. Remove mushrooms. Brown meat in juice from mushrooms. Add seasonings. Add the rest of ingredients except spaghetti. Stir and simmer over low heat about 1 hour. (May be refrigerated or frozen at this point.) Cook spaghetti according to package directions. Mix some of the sauce with drained spaghetti. Serve remaining sauce as topping with additional grated cheese. Serves 25.

Exotic Luncheon Salad

8 cups bite-size pieces of cooked turkey
   or chicken breast
1 can sliced water chestnuts
2 pounds seedless grapes
2 cups sliced celery
1 large can litchi nuts or pineapple chunks
2½ cups salad dressing
½ cup cream, whipped
1 tablespoon lemon juice
¼ teaspoon curry powder
1 teaspoon soy sauce
1 teaspoon sugar
2 cups toasted slivered almonds

In a large mixing bowl, combine the turkey, chestnuts, grapes, celery, and litchi nuts or pineapple chunks. In a separate bowl, combine the salad dressing, whipped cream, lemon juice, curry powder, soy sauce, and sugar. (May be refrigerated in separate bowls, covered, at this point.) Combine turkey mixture with salad dressing mixture; add slivered almonds. Serve in lettuce cups. Serves 25.

Scrambled Eggs for a Crowd

¼ cup butter
¼ cup flour
2 cups milk
3 dozen eggs
1½ cups milk
3 tablespoons salt
1 teaspoon pepper
¼ cup butter, melted

Make white sauce: Melt ¼ cup butter and stir in the flour. Add milk and cook until thickened. Set aside. Beat eggs until fluffy. Add milk, salt, pepper, and ¼ cup melted butter. Cook slowly

in a large heavy kettle until creamy and just beginning to set. Add white sauce and cook, stirring constantly but gently, until eggs are set as desired. These eggs will stay moist 1 to 2 hours, which makes them good for buffet serving. Also delicious with grated cheese stirred in at the last. Serves 20 to 25.

Rice Casserole

¾ cup margarine
2 cups sliced mushrooms
½ cup chopped onion
1 cup chopped celery or almonds
5 cups uncooked rice
½ cup chopped parsley
1 pound cheese, grated
4 quarts water
¼ cup salt
1 teaspoon pepper
2 tablespoons powdered chicken bouillon

Heat butter in a large Dutch oven; add mushrooms, onions, and celery or almonds, and sauté. Add rice, parsley, and cheese. Combine remaining ingredients and pour over rice mixture. Pour into two 9" x 13" x 2" baking pans. Bake at 375° F. for 45 minutes to 1 hour. Serves 50. *Note:* Casserole may be refrigerated, then reheated slowly in oven with ½ cup water dribbled over top.

Chicken à la King

8 pounds chicken
8 whole black peppercorns
4 whole cloves
4 whole allspice
2 bay leaves
4 teaspoons salt
2 ribs celery with leaves, chopped
2 carrots, chopped
2 onions, diced
4 cups fresh mushrooms
1⅓ cups fat (part chicken fat, part butter)
4 cups chicken broth
4 cups milk
¾ cup flour

In a large pot cover chicken with water just barely to cover; simmer until tender, about 45 minutes. Lift chicken from liquid, cool, and remove bones and skin. Put bones and skin back into broth and add peppercorns, cloves, allspice, bay leaves, and salt. Simmer until broth has boiled down to approximately 4 cups; strain. To the strained broth add chopped celery, carrots, and onions; cook until tender. In a skillet, heat fat and sauté mushrooms. Remove mushrooms from fat and add to the vegetables and broth. Stir in 2 cups of the milk. Combine the other 2 cups of milk with the flour to make a smooth paste; stir into broth. Bring broth to a boil; cook until smooth and thickened, stirring constantly. Add chicken pieces. (May be refrigerated at this point. Reheat slowly.) Serve hot chicken and sauce over hot cooked rice or toast or in patty shells. Serves 30 to 36.

Ham Casserole

16 cups ground cooked ham
5 cups grated Cheddar cheese
10 cups milk
80 soda crackers (about 2 packets),
    rolled coarsely
⅔ cup melted butter
½ cup Worcestershire sauce
20 hard-boiled eggs, sliced

Combine all ingredients and pat into two 11″ x 17″ x 2″ baking pans. (May be refrigerated or frozen at this point; adjust baking time, if necessary.) Bake at 350° F. for 1 hour. Serves 50.

INDEX